Doggy Days

Dozens and Dozens of Indoor and Outdoor Activities for You and Your Best Friend— Tricks and Games, Arts and Crafts, Stories and Songs, and Much More!

Joe and Melanie Borgenicht

TEN SPEED PRESS
Berkeley / Toronto

A Kirsty Melville Book

Ten Speed Press
P.O. Box 7123
Berkeley, California 94707
www.tenspeed.com

Distributed in Canada by Ten Speed Press Canada.

Design by Susan Van Horn
Illustrations by Alexander Stadler

A Quirk Book
www.quirkproductions.com

Library of Congress Cataloging-in-Publication Data
Borgenicht, Joe.
Doggy days : dozens and dozens of indoor and outdoor activities for you and
your best friend : tricks and games, arts and crafts, stories and songs,
and much more! / by Joe and Melanie Borgenicht.
p. cm.
ISBN 1-58008-323-4
1. Dogs--Exercise. 2. Dogs--Equipment and supplies. 3. Handicraft.
I. Borgenicht, Melanie. II. Title.
SF427.45 .B67 2001
636.7'08937--dc21
2001002083

First printing, 2001
Printed in Singapore

1 2 3 4 5 6 7 8 9 10—04 03 02 01

Contents

Introduction

"There are some simple truths,
and the dogs know what they are."
—JOSEPH DUEMER

Of course, then there are some not-so-simple truths . . . and every dog owner wants to know those, too. With the help of this book, you will either learn your dog's simple truths, or make your dog as neurotic as you are.

Either way, it will bring the two of you closer together.

Why? Because our doggies are the foundations of our families. They let us share their bedrooms, they try to take us for walks at least twice a day, and they greet us excitedly at the door whether we've been gone for five days or five minutes. Like the old proverb says, "Time spent loving your dog cannot be deducted from your life"—or something like that.

Who among us wants to live a day without our dog? Well, a day or two wouldn't hurt that much . . . just remember that in doggy time, two days is nearly two weeks. Which means two hours is really about a half a day to a dog. Just think of how easy it would be to spend four hours (an entire dog day!) with your pooch and how happy you'd both be at the end of it!

Dogs have so much to teach us. They teach us that unconditional love can come in a furry, four-legged package. They teach us that it's fun to roll in the mud and chase the mailman—though not necessarily in that order. They teach us that wherever we are is the perfect place to plop down, and that naps are always a good idea. They teach us that you don't need a TV when you have a bay window.

This book is designed to help you and your doggy spend the most enjoyable day, half-day, or half-hour possible. Maybe you'll cook together, play together, and celebrate together. You'll be inside together, be outside together, or be upside-down together. You'll learn how to make all kinds of doggy necessities, prizes, and toys. But mainly, you'll learn how to make the most of your quality time with your dog.

So enjoy! Grab a bone, pull up your pillow, and . . .

Carpe dog-em!

Artsy Days

Whether your dog has the handyman skills of Rufus Vila or the creative crafting of Bella Stewart, the activities in this section are great ways to spend time together. Not only will you be making doghouses and clothing for your pooch, but you'll also learn to make holiday cards and to paint with your pet. You'll learn how to write poems and songs, create scrapbooks and photo albums, and make toys and ID tags for your dog to wear.

Artsy days are for both you and your doggy to create gifts, tools, and toys for the two of you and your doggy friends.

Projects to Do for Your Dog

Build a Doghouse

Whether your dog stays indoors or roams the outdoors, a doghouse can benefit both of you. If he is primarily an outdoor dog, the benefits are obvious. A doghouse will provide him shelter from the elements and a safe place to sleep during the night.

Even if he is an indoor dog, a doghouse is still a great spot for hanging out when he's outside. It's a place for him to store bones and balls—a place from which he can watch the world around him. It also helps you as the owner because you'll know exactly where to go when your left slipper goes missing. (It also gives husbands some shelter when they've done the wrong thing.)

Before you build a doghouse, there are a few hard-and-fast doggy standards that you should know.

Size matters. Industry and veterinary standards recommend that a doghouse not be too big. A doghouse large enough for Rufus to turn around and lay down in is sufficient.

Neatness counts. A doghouse built in a hurry or by cutting corners could endanger your dog's life. Be thoughtful when you select materials—the chemicals used in pressure-treated lumber can be toxic to your dog. Take care when you hammer nails and drill screws, since any exposed, sharp points can hurt a doggy's tender paw.

Note: The plans for the following doghouse are very basic and written for the owner of a medium-sized dog.

WHAT YOU'LL NEED:

Materials:

- 1 2″ x 4″ x 10′ pressure-treated lumber piece
- 1 4′ x 8′ piece (at least ¹/₂″ thick) of exterior-grade plywood sheathing
- 1 small box 16 penny framing nails
- 1 small box 1 ¹/₂″ yellow zinc deck screws
- 1 small box roofing nails
- 10 sheets of shingles
- 1 small can exterior-grade paint

Tools:

- Tape measure
- Circular saw or handsaw
- Jigsaw
- Drill
- Hammer
- File

Diagram A: 2″ x 4″ x 10′ pressure-treated lumber

Rim	Side	Side	Back	Front	
24″	24″	24″	21″	21″	

WHAT YOU'LL DO:

1. Lay out your plywood sheathing and lumber. Using diagrams A and C, measure, mark, and label all the material in pencil. Frame pieces are to be made out of the pressure-treated lumber, while Wall, Roof, and Floor pieces will be cut out of the plywood sheathing. Remember: measure twice, cut once!

2. Make all of your cuts and then lay out the pieces.

3. Construct the Base Frame of your doghouse. Nail the pressure-treated two-by-fours together as shown in diagram B to create a Base Frame.

4. Attach the Floor piece to the Base Frame. Lay the Base Frame on a flat surface. Using deck screws, attach the plywood floor to the Base Frame. The plywood should sit atop the frame.

5. Using deck screws, attach Side Walls to the side pieces of the Base Frame.

6. Using deck screws, attach the Front and Back Walls to the Base Frame. If any screw tips are exposed inside, file them smooth.

7. Using the framing nails, attach the single Roof Rim two-by-four so that it connects the peaks of the Front and Back Walls. See diagram D for proper

Diagram B: Base Frame

Back Frame

Side Frame

Side Frame

Front Frame

Diagram C: 4' x 8' Exterior-Grade
Plywood Sheathing

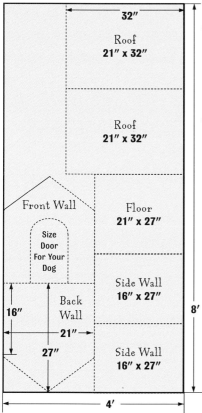

orientation of the piece. Ensure no part of the Roof Rim sticks out beyond the peaks.

8. Using deck screws, attach the Left Roof and Right Roof to the Roof Rim. The plywood roof pieces should extend beyond the front, back, and side of the doghouse evenly.

9. Using roofing nails, attach the shingles. Start at the bottom and work your way to the top. Be sure to use a staggered "brick" pattern and overlap the shingles by a few inches. This allows water to flow down the shingles and not into the house. When you get to the peak from both sides, fold a course over the top so that water will flow down each side.

Diagram D: Attach Roof Rim

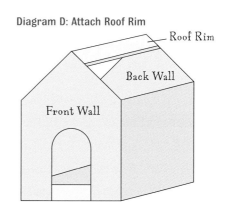

Great! You've got a doghouse! To add some finishing touches, paint the outside and lay a piece of carpet or cushion inside for your dog.

Doggy Clothing

The world of doggy clothing is a world unto itself. As far as we know, Vera Wang has yet to design an evening gown for little Bella, but what's stopping you? Most dog owners either love doggy clothes or hate them. You'll find out soon enough how Bella feels about them!

For doggy clothes lovers: Today you'll learn how to make a doggy jacket. That's right: you and Bella will do it together. No, the two of you won't be driving down to the pet store to buy a raincoat. This garb will come from the heart.

For doggy clothes haters: Why not make a doggy jacket to give to your neighbor's dog? Just think of the fun you'll have watching that German Shepherd prance down the street in a Bella original.

You can customize this doggy jacket by choosing special material, designs, and fabric. Denim is a good, sturdy material that makes for a really hip dog (and it doesn't wear out as much as other fabrics).

There are two styles of doggy clothing: male and female. Male clothing should not extend all the way back to his tail because of the way he goes "number one." Female clothing can go all the way, however. You will see adjustments in the directions depending on which style you are sewing.

WHAT YOU'LL NEED:

- Sewing machine or needle and thread
- Material
- Flexible tailor's tape
- Wax pencil or crayon
- Scissors

MEASURING YOUR DOG:

With a flexible tailor's tape:

1. Measure around your dog's neck. (A)

2. Measure from the base of your dog's neck to the base of the tail. (B) Subtract 5 inches if your dog is male.

3. Measure from the front of your dog's neck, along the belly, to the front of the back legs. (C) Subtract 5 inches if your dog is male.

4. Measure from your dog's back to the top of the front legs. (D)

5. Measure around your dog's front legs near the body. (E)

6. Finally, measure around the widest point on your dog's chest. (F)

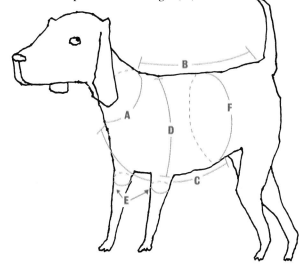

WHAT YOU'LL DO:

1. Transfer the measurements to your material using a wax pencil or crayon and draw the outline of the jacket. Cut out the material.

9

2. Hem the edges of the leg holes by folding approximately one half-inch up and sewing across.

3. Sew velcro strips along both sides, following the outline of the jacket.

4. Lay the jacket on your dog's back. Fasten the velcro to make the sleeves and to connect the jacket around her waist.

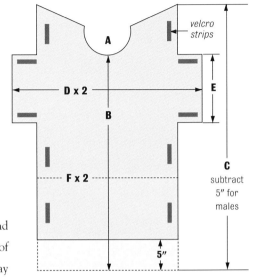

   To enhance her jacket, sew lace around the neck and leg edges or add patches of other material shapes to the sides. You may also want to make a winter version of the jacket out of heavier material.

Other Doggy Clothes Ideas:

Cut down one of your worn-out sweatshirts.

Hem up one of your worn-out skirts.

Place an old pair of socks on your dog's feet for booties.

Cut ear holes in an old hat and fit on your dog's head.

Pretty soon, you'll have a regular fashion hound!

Dog Toys and Gifts

ID Tags

WHAT YOU'LL NEED:

- Paper
- Markers
- Laminating sheets (available at office supply stores)

- Hole punch
- String
- Computer and printer (optional)

DOG LICENSE

Name: .... State: ....

Address: ....

....

Phone Number: ....

Estimated Date of Birth: ....

Eyes: .... Hair: .... Size: □Sm. □Med. □Lg.

Favorite Food: ....

Restrictions: ....

In case of emergency call: ....

Vet: ....

Place Picture Here

WHAT YOU'LL DO:

Make a dog license, and Bella will carry photo ID just like you carry your driver's license! Model the doggy license on the template on page 11. Create a small card (using your computer or, if it's legible, your own handwriting) with all the information in place. Paste on a picture of your dog and laminate the card. Punch a hole in one side and attach it to Bella's collar with string.

Add a religious icon like a cross or star of David to your dog's license for some extra spiritual protection. That is, if she believes. . . .

If you just don't have the time to make this yourself, look for a store that sells dog tags that you can personalize. Just fill out the form and watch someone etch Bella's name into a piece of thin metal shaped like a bone.

Collars

Making a collar for your doggy can be a challenge. If your sewing skills leave something to be desired, don't fret. After making several new collars you'll be a master. The more you practice, the better you get. Try making a new collar at the beginning of every dog year!

WHAT YOU'LL NEED:

- Nylon or cloth collar (available at pet supply stores)
- Sewing machine with embroidery stitch or needle and embroidery thread
- Cloth
- Wax pencil or crayon

BEFORE YOU START:

First, practice. On a drop cloth or other thick material, write out your dog's name and phone number using the wax pencil or crayon. Embroider the practice cloth. The turns are the toughest parts.

WHAT YOU'LL DO:

Once you feel confident, draw out your dog's name and phone number on the nylon collar using the wax pencil or crayon.

Embroider the collar (by hand or with a sewing machine).

The better you get, the more you can do. Try adding an image of a bone or a flower to your dog's collar.

If you don't have the time to embroider and the kids are about to go off to summer camp, get *them* to make the collar. Instead of making ugly leather belts, they can stamp out their dog's name on a short piece of leather. Most summer camps will have leather-stamping tools, but if you want to do this at home you can find everything you need at a craft store.

Toys

Toys are the easiest things you can make for your dog. As far as your dog is concerned, whatever he gets hold of and you grab away is a toy. But if you want to be a bit more creative, here are some ideas:

Old socks bunched together. There's nothing better.

Thrift store pillows. Small pillows are a blast for dogs to chew apart.

1/2″-thick surgical tubing about 2 feet long. Believe it or not this is one of the funniest things we've ever seen our dog play with.

Homemade fleece. With a little fabric from the fabric store and some stuffing, you can quickly sew together an original chew toy. It's much cheaper than buying one in the store, and it lasts longer. As soon as your doggy chews a hole in it you can sew it right back up!

Projects to Do with Your Dog

Doggy Painting

Any day is a good doggy painting day—and by doggy painting we mean both painting on your dog and teaching your dog to paint.

Whether you're going for the best doggy costume prize in a local canine parade, are thinking about opening an Animal Art Gallery, or are just looking to kill a few hours with Rufus, doggy painting is fun for everyone.

WHAT YOU'LL NEED:

- Children's bath paint
- Paintbrushes

BEFORE YOU START:

As with most wet materials, it is important that the paint doesn't get into your dog's eyes. And even though these paints are non-toxic, try to keep your dog from licking or otherwise ingesting them.

Because the painting can get messy, you may want to do this somewhere that is paint-safe—outside, in the bathroom, or over a tarp.

WHAT YOU'LL DO:

Once you get your paints, mark a small area on your dog's paw, let it dry, and then wash it off just to be sure that the paints will work on his fur and skin. Now you're ready to paint your dog! Don't worry: Children's bath paints will wash right off with soap and water.

Be ingenious, or use one of these great "theme" ideas:

"Blue Dog" Dog/Smurf Dog. The best part of painting your dog entirely blue is that he'll look like a Smurf, but he won't talk in that high, squeaky voice.

Camouflage Dog. In three shades of green, your dog will disappear into any bush, shrub, or jungle.

Candy-Cane Dog. White and red stripes make for a great holiday doggy.

"Clifford the Big Red Dog" Dog. A bright coat of red makes your dog into many children's literary hero.

Jack-o'-Dog. A base coat of orange and a toothy black grin on your dog's side makes for a scary Halloween doggy.

Jackson Pollock Dog. A splattering of many different colors of paint makes your dog into a work of art!

Polka Dot Dog. Polka dots of any color work well alone, or, if your dog loves being painted, you could start with a base coat and then add spots. Turn your dog into a Dalmatian using white and black! A purple base with yellow spots makes a great H. R. Puffinstuff character! A base coat of red with black dots makes for a lucky ladybug.

Skunk Dog. A streak of white down the back of a black dog makes for an excellent look.

Tiger Dog. Put a few brown lines down the sides of a tan dog to create a scary look.

Tube-Sock Dog. A white base coat with three red stripes on his rear end makes Rufus look like his favorite thing to steal from your laundry hamper.

VW Dog. This design gets its name from the "Peace" and "Love" symbols you'll paint on Rufus's sides. If he enjoys being painted, why not try an orange base coat?

Salvador Doggy

If your pooch doesn't like to be paint*ed*, maybe he would enjoy paint*ing*. Some animals love to paint. Monkeys use their hands, and elephants use their trunks, so why shouldn't dogs use their tails!

WHAT YOU'LL NEED:

- Children's bath paint
- Poster board
- String or (easily removable) masking tape
- Drop cloth or old sheet

WHAT YOU'LL DO:

We recommend using one of these two methods.

Brush Tail. If your dog doesn't mind, dip his tail in some paint, hold a piece of poster board behind his tail, and pet him fiercely. You'll find that the more you love him, the grander the artwork!

Tail Brush. Tape or tie a paint brush to your dog's tail. Dip the brush in paint, hold up a poster board, and pet him fiercely.

Good luck! Even the drop cloth might be an abstract masterpiece.

Dog Prints

Prints make a great addition to a scrapbook/photo album, especially if you start when your pooch is just a puppy (see Making and Keeping a Doggy Journal/Scrapbook, p. 21).

WHAT YOU'LL NEED:

- Children's bath paint
- Poster board, paper, and/or parchment

WHAT YOU'LL DO:

Dip your dog's paw in a small amount of children's bath paint. Carefully press onto the poster board and let dry.

Easy enough. Maybe you'd like to try these techniques as well:

Follow the paw-print road! Roll out parchment paper and have your dog walk out a trail of doggy prints for your children to follow.

Mark a paw print next to your child's handprint (or your own!). Record their ages. Do this yearly. Frame the prints and hang them in the mudroom so Bella's leash has a special place right next to your child's coat hook!

A T-shirt covered in paw prints also makes a great birthday, Mother's Day, or Father's Day gift (see Decorating T-Shirts, p. 20).

Holiday Cards

WHAT YOU'LL NEED:

- Camera
- Film
- Stationery
- Photo album corners
- Calligraphy pen

WHAT YOU'LL DO:

Why send the usual holiday card of your dog and Santa, when you're not even in the picture? Those are cute, but common. Be original and make your own!

For a "classier" doggy holiday card, purchase some black-and-white film. Try taking several pictures of your entire family (your dog is family, after all) in the snow or in front of a fire—whatever your heart and holiday desires.

Once you have your photo, make copies and mount them onto stationery. Use photo corners to show just how much you and Bella care.

With your calligraphy pen in hand, fill your card with a doggy slogan. Here are a few ideas to get you started:

"I hope you get all the bones you want this Christmas!"

"Celebrate the Holiday Season: Lay around as much as possible, go for a walk once a day, and eat all the leftovers you can handle."

"This year, we're going to celebrate the holidays doggy style!"

Decorating T-Shirts

With a little T-shirt paint (found in craft stores), you can make up some great clothes for both you and Rufus to wear.

WHAT YOU'LL NEED:

- T-shirt paint
- Plain cotton T-shirts (in sizes to fit friends, family, and your dog)
- Paintbrushes

WHAT YOU'LL DO:

Paint fabulous gifts to give to family and friends! Try these ideas for starters:

His-and-Hers Doggy Shirts. Try painting a portrait of your dog on a T-shirt for you and a portrait of yourself on a T-shirt for your dog!

Paw Prints for Father's Day. Use the doggy prints technique above (see Dog Prints, p. 18) to cover a T-shirt for Dad with Rufus's "signature." Then let Rufus carry it to him on Father's Day.

Costume Shirt. If you don't like the idea of painting on your dog directly (see Doggy Painting, p. 15), try painting a T-shirt for your dog to wear.

Doggy Skeleton. Paint your dog's skeleton in white on a black T-shirt for a classic Halloween shirt.

Making and Keeping a Doggy Journal/Scrapbook

"Mem-ries . . . of the dogs that are mine . . . " (The song goes something like that, doesn't it?) When it comes to keeping memories of your beloved pooch, nothing beats a complete doggy scrapbook.

When it's done right, your scrapbook will carry the best memories of your best friend for years after she has gone to doggy heaven. But let's not think about that . . .

The best part about recording memories is making them!

WHAT YOU'LL NEED:

- A sketchbook or large journal
- Photo album corners
- Plastic bags
- Doggy mementos

WHAT YOU'LL DO:

Since everyone's doggy is unique, every doggy scrapbook will be different, but here are a few ideas to get you started:

Cover. Paint, draw, or write your doggy's name on the front cover of your book. Be creative, adding a favorite picture or a collage of her leftover chew toys. Or let Bella paint a picture for the cover (see Salvador Doggy, p. 17)!

Page 1. List your dog's physical information: height, weight, name, date of birth, and inked paw print.

Page 2. Write the story of how you and your dog came to find each other.

Page 3. Stick on pictures of your dog as a puppy. If you don't have any younger photos, try drawing what she might have looked like back then.

Page 4. Describe your pup's favorite toys, and tell stories of nostalgic trinkets that she doesn't play with anymore—an old favorite shoe, a dilapidated old favorite ball, and so forth. Then put them in a plastic bag to attach to the book.

Page 5. Hunk/babe page. Place a picture of your dog's favorite dog idol. Lassie? Beethoven? Someone from the park?

Page 6. Favorite sayings. If your dog could speak English, what would she say?

You can carry on from here . . . adding pictures, stories, and memorabilia from throughout your dog's life. Add photos from your hikes and treasures from your road trips. You can add a doggy health page detailing the trials and tribulations of Bella's trips to the doctor. Pages of photos ordered chronologically fit beautifully into the middle of any scrapbook. Don't forget to add captions and dates.

It's also fun to chronicle your doggy's life over time. On her birthday every year, make a pawprint in the book to record her growth and add notes about other changes. Once the print starts to look the same, you can use different colored paint!

Make it fun. Make it last. Because you can never go back, but you can always remember.

Fine Art Fun with Your Dog

Singing Together

With a little training, your dog will sing along with you. Some dogs take to singing naturally. They love to hear the sounds of the notes and often will bark right in!

The best way to begin to teach your dog to sing is to first teach her to speak. As you train her, give her a hand command so that you can use your voice for singing. Once she's got that down, the two of you are ready to sing.

You can sing any song with your dog. The best way to approach it is to replace a common word in the chorus of a song with a "woof" for your dog to sing. For example "Every Little Woof She Does Is Magic," or "Woof, in the USA."

Songs to Sing to Your Dog

Who doesn't love to be serenaded? Don't let your dog fool you—if she walks away from you in the middle of your high note, it just means she wants you to follow her and sing louder. At least that's what we like to think. Feel free to change the lyrics, names, or events to suit your dog.

"Birds, Glorious Birds"

(to the tune of "Food, Glorious Food")

Birds, glorious birds,
Oh how I could eat them.
Birds, glorious birds,
How I love to chase them.
Blue jays and orange-breasted ones,
Brown finches and sparrows.
Mom, please fill that suet cage,
So there's more there to choose from.

"Ladle, Ladle, Ladle"

(to the tune of "Dreidl, Dreidl, Dreidl")

I have a wooden ladle,
I found it on the stoop.
Mommy must have dropped it
After making chicken soup.

Oh ladle, ladle, ladle
You are my favorite tchotchke,
I can't wait 'til tomorrow
Cause mommy's making latke.

That's the idea! Now make up one of your own for your dog.

If it's bedtime, try one of these lullabies. Just insert your dog's name and sing yourself silly.

"Hush Little Bella"

(to the tune of "Hush Little Baby")

Hush Little Bella, don't bark a word,
Papa's gonna buy you a yummy bird.

And if that yummy bird gets out,
Papa's gonna find you a cat and mouse.

And if that cat and mouse don't play,
Papa's gonna take you to the park all day.

And if that doggy park is bare,
Papa's gonna chase you around like a hare.

And if that chase doesn't tire you out,
Papa will drive you around and about.

And if that drive doesn't do the trick,
Papa will pretend that he is sick.

So hush Little Bella, don't bark a peep,
Papa doesn't feel well—he's asleep.

"Rufus the Puppy"

(to the tune of "Rock-a-bye Baby")

Rufus the puppy
Peed in the house.
Now he knows better
And he wants out.
Whine at the window,
Beg at the door,
'Til someone comes running,
At quarter to four.

"My Favorite Things"

(to the tune of "My Favorite Things")

Slippers and papers and big furry mittens,
Blue socks and red socks, why, you smell
    like kittens.
Treats from the table and treats from the stove,
I don't feel so well—that tasted like clove.

Chew toys and new toys and kids walking by,
Sitting, and lying, and watching the sky.
Mailmen and milkmen, they make me so mad,
Why do they keep coming back to my pad?

Dancing with Your Dog

Many circuses feature dogs who dance around the ring, but few dog owners would subject their pooches to that kind of humiliation. It doesn't take much to teach your dog to dance around the house, but who wants to dance alone?

The challenge and the fun is dancing together!

For those of us who were forced to take ballroom dancing in our youth, we've probably already got down dancing with our dog. For those of you who don't even know what the fox trot is, we'll start fresh.

Dancing with your dog is a great way for the two of you to stay close and active, but be aware of Bella's abilities before "tripping the light fantastic" together:

Size matters. If you have a big dog and you can hold her weight, have her lean against you in a bear hug. If you have a small dog, feel free to pick her up by her front paws and gently spin her around the yard. Be extra careful with medium-sized dogs, as they don't have the reach to lean against your waist and they weigh too much to be carried around. When dancing with your medium-sized dog, use a hands-off method and just step together—she on her hind feet, you on yours.

Watch for pulled muscles. Don't move too fast if your dog decides to join you. She'll only be working with two feet, and those two feet mean she'll move even slower than those of us who have two left feet. Take it slowly and don't move suddenly.

Now you're ready to dance:

Play some music. We recommend swing, big band, or Dixieland Jazz, but use whatever you like.

Formal Dancing: The Dog-Trot. With the first beat of the music, take one step toward Bella with your left foot as she moves back. With the second beat, take another step toward Bella with your right foot. She should move back. On the third beat, take one step to your left. On the fourth beat, bring your right foot together with your left. She should follow. Repeat, and don't forget to smile!

Fun Dancing: The Funky Kitten. Get on all fours next to your dog. On the first beat of music, meow to get her attention. On the second beat, arch your back like a cat who's on the defensive. On the third beat, hiss. On the fourth beat, arch your back. Repeat. Take it from us—it may sound ridiculous, but Bella will love to see you move like this.

Solo Dancing. All kinds of fun can be had with your favorite music and your dog. Just let yourself go and let Bella join in. Try a little break dancing. Try some Russian dancing. If Bella has some friends over, try the Hokey Pokey.

Writing Stories about Your Dog

What better way to capture your dog's life than by writing about it! A picture may say a thousand words, but a thousand words may paint a better picture—especially when it comes to your beloved four-legged friend.

For this activity, we'll make a children's book for your children, your dog, or your bookshelf.

WHAT YOU'LL NEED:

- 8 1/2" x 11" construction paper and plain white paper
- 8 1/2" x 11" poster board
- Pens
- Glue
- A story about your dog

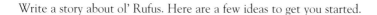

WHAT YOU'LL DO:

Write a story about ol' Rufus. Here are a few ideas to get you started.

Fairy Tale. Start with "Woof upon a time . . ."

A Dog's Life. Start with "One day, Rufus was very blue. His owner, Mel, left on her way to wherever it is she goes everyday." Next, think about what your dog might do all day while you're gone and write about it.

Bedtime. Start with "Rufus was plumb tuckered out. Another long day filled with breakfast, a walk, a nap, some treats, a nap (interrupted by the guy in the brown uniform dropping off boxes), another nap, a greeting at the front door, another nap, dinner and a movie, and another nap had just about done it for him." How does he prepare for bed? Write about it.

Whatever the story, it's sure to be a hit. Once you've got it down, separate it into equal sections—one or two paragraphs or sentences per page.

Fold your plain white paper in halves—like a book—and rewrite or type your story onto the pages.

Add illustrations. Use pens to draw pictures for each page or cut out images from construction paper and glue them onto the pages.

Once you've got your pages together, think up a title and copy it onto a cover made of poster board cut to size and folded in half. Here are some potential titles:

Rufus's Big Day
Rufus and the Magic Bone
Rufus and the Rotten Slipper
Rufus and the Big, Long, Nap
Rufus and the Smelly, Stinky, Stuck-up, Selfish, Snobby, Snooty Cat

Once you've finished your storybook, try reading it to Rufus. He'll love it—or at least he'll love to hear you say his name over and over again.

Dog-gerel: Writing Poems

The poor dog, in life is the firmest friend,
The first to welcome, foremost to defend,
Whose honest heart is still the master's own,
Who labours, fights, lives, breathes for him alone,
Unhonour'd falls, unnoticed all his worth,
Denied in heaven the soul he held on earth,
While man, vain insect hopes to be forgiven,
And claims himself a sole exclusive heaven.
—Lord Byron, inscription on the monument of his
Newfoundland dog, 1808

Although poetry is more enjoyable for us than for our dog, it will still entertain and bring us closer to him. As we grow to understand and appreciate a dog's loyalty, love, and needs, perhaps we will gain a new appreciation for his best qualities.

Try to write a few poems of your own. Start with a haiku. The first and third lines have five syllables and the second has seven. It's fun and easy!

Dog at Bedtime
Lying on your bed
Making warm and soft and nice
Where your feet will go.

Dog in the Morning
Waiting for breakfast.
Still waiting for yummy food.
Get Up! Lazy fool!

See! Once you've mastered writing haiku, try one that's more free-form. Remember, poems don't have to rhyme.

If you want to write a poem especially for reading to your dog, try ending each line with a word that she knows—you'll keep her interest that way. Here's one that works for us:

BELLA you chase the BIRDS
Like a writer chases words.
Sometimes it's a KITTY
That makes you look all gritty.
Once it was a BABY
Who made you all kinds of crazy.
But if you're good and you SIT
We might let you chew on our mitt.
After you swallow this TREAT
We'll give you dinner to EAT.
GOOD DOG!

You get the picture. She loves it!

Dog Photography and Videography

There are always stories to tell about the time that Rufus grabbed the ten-pound holiday ham off the counter and carried it into the backyard. Or the time that he slept upside-down on the couch.

They're great stories to share, and we've all got them. So why not make the memories more lasting by capturing them on film?

Portraits

These techniques can be used to take portraits that you can frame for your mantle, send out on a holiday card, or add to your doggy journal/scrapbook.

WHAT YOU'LL NEED:

- A camera
- Film

OPTIONAL:

- 1 4' x 8' sheet of waferboard
- A jigsaw
- Paint

WHAT YOU'LL DO:

Puppy Portraits. The best time in a dog's life is his youth. And who doesn't want to remember when Rufus was at his cutest? Take a portrait of Rufus every month for the first year of his life. Once the chronology is complete, put the pictures in a multi-picture frame or into his scrapbook.

Studio Portraits. Some photographers allow dogs into their studios. As Rufus gets into his teenage years, take him to a photograpy studio and dress him up. By the time he's a dog-year teen, you'll know his personality well enough to know what costume suits him best. Is he a cowboy or garbage man?

Do-It-Yourself Studio. Dress Rufus up using some of the costume techniques in "Halloween," on page 113 and set up your own photo shoot. These pictures are great for holiday cards or just to show around the dog park (especially if you want to embarrass Rufus).

Trading Places. Here's a photo opportunity just like the one at the carnival! Using a jigsaw, cut two holes—one at his height large enough for your head and one at your height large enough for a dog's head—out of a four-by-eight sheet of waferboard. Paint your body under the doggy hole, and Rufus's body under the human hole (you may need a stool for your pooch to sit on, behind the board). Stick your heads in, and smile while a friend takes the picture. This is also a great party favor for doggy birthday parties!

Live Action

WHAT YOU'LL NEED:

- A video camera
- Film

WHAT YOU'LL DO:

Fill your video library with home videos of every milestone in your doggy's life. Guests love to watch these types of videos, after all!

First Times. Take shots of your doggy's birth—if you are fortunate enough to be there—or the first time you laid eyes on him at the pound. Be sure to keep the camera rolling for the first time he pees in the house, and the first time he pees outside. But don't stop there! Record his first bone, his first slipper, his first doghouse, his first trip to the dog park, and his first girlfriend—he'll love to watch these videos again and again.

Doggy Life Moments. Once you've lived with your pooch for a while, you'll get to know his routine inside and out. You know he barks when the mailman comes—capture it on film. You know he jumps on the bed every morning when the alarm goes off—film that, too. You know he comes to find you everyday at five—you and your camera can be waiting around the corner.

Once you've got your photos or videos together, post them on a website for the world to enjoy!

Outdoors-y Days

Whether you're the owner of Rufus Appleseed or Bella Bly, staying indoors all day just won't cut it. Outside is where a doggy loves to be—aside from her other favorite place, which is under your feet.

Outside, you and your pooch can chase birds, cats, and mailmen. Outside, you and your pooch can chew newspapers and roll in snow and grass. Outside, you and your pooch can mark new territory, run like the wind, and dive into the water like Rufus Louganis.

The "Outdoors-y Days" chapter shows you how to make the most of any environment with your pooch. Here you'll find games, tricks, and new doggy sports to strengthen the bond between you and your four-legged loved one.

Games

When it comes to games and tricks, being outdoors with your pooch takes on a whole new meaning. After all, outside it's definitely a dog's world!

If you can get your friends and your friends' dogs to join in, outdoor games can be even more fun. Here you'll find ideas for games you can play with your dog and games you can play with your dog and his friends.

Racing Games

To the Tree and Back

"To the Tree and Back" pits you and your dog against each other. You can create a variation so you and Rufus can compete together against his friends (and their owners).

WHAT YOU'LL NEED:

- A clear stretch of ground about fifteen to twenty yards long, with a tree at one end

- Running shoes

WHAT YOU'LL DO:

Race!

Stand fifteen to twenty yards away from the tree with Rufus. Mark the location with your backpack, or pick a spot that's easy to locate (a rock, a trash can). This is point A. Run together to the tree. Then run back to point A.

Easy enough. If you beat your dog, you win!

Variation: Doubles. Compete as teams against friends and their dogs. The team to return to point A first wins!

Tips and Tricks:

When racing with your dog against other teams, try to keep him focused on you. Get his attention a few moments before you change directions. Make sure that he doesn't stop at the tree to sniff out who was racing there yesterday.

Fetching Games

Most dogs love to fetch just about anything—as long as it doesn't involve shots from the vet. From sticks to balls, the newspaper to your slippers, rubber toys to rubber bands, your dog can have fun for hours playing fetch.

We like to think that our dogs are playing with us. But in a dog's reality, we are not throwing the stick for them to bring back. They are bringing us the stick to see how far we can throw it.

Regardless of who is playing with whom, fetching games can go on for as long as your arm holds out.

The Fastest Fetcher in the West . . . or the East

This game tests your dog's speed and ability to retrieve an object, and is played with two or more dogs. If you only have one dog, find a friend who has a dog and go to the park together!

WHAT YOU'LL NEED:

- Whatever your dog likes to fetch (rubber chew toys, sticks, tennis balls)
- A stopwatch

WHAT YOU'LL DO:

If there's someone with you who's dogless, designate him as the master timer, who will time each dog's retrieval of the object. Otherwise, one person can do it—but someone else will have to take over when the timer is busy throwing an object for his dog!

Owners should throw the object for their own dog. The clock stops when the dog drops the object at the feet of her owner. Whichever dog has the fastest time gets to keep the object! Each dog should take her turn, one dog at a time, or the game will quickly turn into The Biggest Dog in the Park.

Frisbee Games

Some dogs take to playing Frisbee better than others. If your dog likes disk, then you've got an easy time entertaining in the park.

Try these games:

Keep-Away. You and a friend throw the Frisbee back and forth. Your dog gets a good workout running in circles.

Ultimate Frisbee. If your dog, your friends, and your friends' dogs like to play Frisbee, you can alter the rules of Ultimate Frisbee for a big human-and-dog game.

Most Frisbee Catches. With ten Frisbees and several competing dogs, you can stage a contest to see who can make the most catches. Give each dog an individual opportunity to catch all of the Frisbees thrown by her owner. Throw them one after another so that Bella doesn't have time to bring them back between throws. Whichever dog catches the most Frisbees wins!

Tricks

You *can* teach a new dog old tricks. Better still, you can teach a new dog new tricks. In fact, with a little time and energy, you can even teach a middle-aged or old dog new tricks.

Doggy technology hasn't changed that much over the years. So as long as your dog has down the basics (i.e., "sit," "stay," "come"), you can twist your pup's knowledge into some fun and exciting tricks.

Generally, when it comes to training your dog, the biggest hurdle to overcome is communication. We don't have all the answers for training all kinds of dogs. You alone know your dog best, but these are some training guidelines to help in the meantime.

Keep in mind when training your dog, new or old:

Stay positive. Saying, "good boy," giving a treat, or patting him on the head is ten times more effective than a single swat on the rump. Think of it this way: If you didn't speak Italian and you were in Italy asking a waiter for a specific pasta dish, you wouldn't smack him if he didn't understand you right away.

Break it down. Most training can be broken down into sub-tricks. Choose one word for each sub-trick. For example, if you want your dog to fetch your newspaper and bring it to you in bed, then teach him to "get" the paper. Next, teach him to "come" into the bedroom with it. Finally, teach him to "drop" the paper at your bedside. It's much more effective (and less frustrating!) if you take it one step at a time.

Keep it fun. Keep it simple and practice, practice, practice, but if your dog is not having fun, then you probably aren't either. Take a break from training or practice and go play in the yard for a while.

Great! Now that you've decided to teach your dog some tricks, it's time to decide what to teach him. To begin, it's a good idea to start with something that is within his repertoire. If he likes your shoes, teach him to go and get them for you. If he likes to follow you around, teach him to play "sleuth" and drop to the ground every time you turn around.

Here are some other ideas.

Look both ways before crossing the street. Some folks may laugh, but better safe then sorry. Teach your pooch to look left and then right. If no cars are coming, then he can cross. Use this trick to educate your kids, too!

Deliver a drink at a barbeque. Someone has to stay at the grill and watch the chicken. So while you're busy cooking, send Rufus to fetch a cold beverage from the cooler. Once your friends see this trick, he may be working all night, but he'll love the attention.

Fetch your tools. Every handyperson needs a helper. Rufus can learn to grab you a hammer or hand you a screwdriver. Note: If you have trouble teaching him which tool is which, you could fit him with a lightweight tool belt. Then all he has to learn is "come."

Meet a mate. Train Rufus to run up to a specified stranger and follow or sit by them until the stranger pets him. A dog is a great conversation starter, and if you meet the right person you can tell your grandkids it was fate—or at least Rufus—that brought you together.

Swimming

There are dogs that would love to go in the water every day and there are dogs that wouldn't get their feet wet if you paid them in liver treats. Accordingly, there are many different kinds of swimming for you to do with your dog.

WHAT YOU'LL NEED:

- A stream, pool, or lake (for ocean swimming, see At the Beach, p. 48)
- Dog swimming harness or flotation jacket (for beginners)

WHAT YOU'LL DO:

For those dogs who think that water is for drinking, there is wading in a shallow stream.

If you live in the flatlands or a large urban city, you'll probably be able to find public parks with shallow streams running through them. Fountains also work well.

Take your dog to the edge of the water. Try throwing a ball or a stick into the water and see if your dog will fetch it. If she doesn't, walk into the shallow water yourself. If your dog doesn't follow, take her by the collar a few steps into the stream and stand with her. Be sure to pet and console her if she is scared.

After several visits, your dog will be much more comfortable in the water. She may even go the entire length of the walk in the water.

For more daring dogs, there are pools. If you don't have a pool of your own, some communities even have a dog-friendly public pool day (generally the day before it's cleaned, when chlorine levels are low).

Some communities tout doggy swimming resorts. For a few dollars you can take Bella

to swim in a large pool for the day. Until you get an idea of how well your dog can swim, you may want to use a swimming harness or floatation jacket to help hold her up.

Swimming in pools can also help your pooch if she has an injured leg. Swim therapy is offered in some communities to help dogs heal. Talk to your vet to find out if your community offers swim therapy.

For more advanced swimmers, lakes are a good option. Until you are sure that your dog is an excellent swimmer, we recommend using a swimming harness or floatation jacket when swimming in a lake.

Keep your dog close to shore. When you throw a stick or a ball into the water, don't throw it out too far. Swim alongside her, at her pace. Don't jump in and swim a mile the first day. Turn around and head back to shore after a short swim. Increase to longer distances as you would for a long walk or run. If you have a friend with a small boat or skiff, have them follow you in case one of you gets tired.

Other Sports

There are lots of sports that you can enjoy along with your dog. If you bend the rules a little bit, your dog can really play anything with you. But, without bending the rules too much, we've selected a few common—and one not so common—sports to play.

Sailing

Beware! Not all dogs are sea dogs. If you've never tried sailing with your dog, we recommend using a swimming harness or floatation jacket until you know how well he can swim and stay on board. In fact, even if Rufus is a great swimmer, it's a good idea to fit him with a floatation harness anyway. Until you are comfortable with his abilities on a boat, keep a close eye on him.

Keep him leashed up in the cabin for the first few trips. After that, the deck is a great place as long as he's a good swimmer.

Running

Most dogs love nothing more than to run by your side for as long as you can take it, but be careful! Behind that smiling, panting, drooling exterior lies the potential for many health problems.

If you're going to run with your dog:

1. **Build up distances. Start small—a half mile or so—and increase from there. As a general rule, a one- or two-mile doggy jog is safe. Anything more than that is not recommended.**

2. **Jog during cooler hours. The hot mid-day sun can be fatal to your dog.**

3. **Be aware of jogging surfaces. Though grass may not be the best surface for you to run on, it is better for your dog, especially when compared to hot asphalt or hard cement.**

4. Take plenty of water, enough for both you and Rufus. Some vets recommend that you not force your dog to drink because it may interfere with his panting—just let him do what he needs to do.

5. Keep control of your dog. There are many leashes available that allow you to run while holding your dog hands-free. Primarily, it's important to keep your dog in front of you and out of traffic.

6. Be aware of your dog's age, breed, and any history of injury. All dogs may be equal, but they are built differently and some are simply more suited to activity than others.

Co-Ed Doggy Stickball

If you have a lot of friends with well-trained dogs—who like chasing balls and bringing them back to you—then co-ed doggy stickball is for you!

WHAT YOU'LL NEED:

- A stickball bat (an old broom end will do) about 4' long
- A bucket of tennis balls (the more the better)
- A baseball diamond
- 10–16 friends
- 5–8 dogs

The rules to co-ed doggy stickball are basically the same as in baseball—with a few exceptions:

1. There *is* crying in doggy stickball.

2. Doggy stickball lasts only four innings—or as long as your bucket of balls holds out.

3. Teams are smaller. Split your group into two teams. Dogs should play on the same team as their owners.

4. It is difficult to get a dog to sit, stay, *and* tag someone on second, so we recommend keeping the humans in the infield. Let the dogs do the long-distance running to the outfield. This works out well in stickball because tennis balls do not go as far as baseballs.

5. Not every team member gets to bat. Unfortunately, until our furrier friends develop an opposable claw, they don't get to hit.

Here's the idea. Note: This is only the idea. The game will depend on how well-trained the dogs are.

1. A human pitches to another human.

2. The batter hits the ball.

3. If the ball is hit in the infield, anyone can get it.

4. If the ball is hit in the outfield, only a dog can retrieve it. He can either bring the ball to his owner, who throws it to a baseman, or he can take the ball directly to the runner's base.

5. Once a team gets three outs, the other team is up at bat. A new inning begins after each team has been at bat.

Tips:

Pick one dog at a time to retrieve the ball. If too many dogs are chasing the ball at once, or all the owners are shouting, all you get is confusion and a lost ball. The dog's owner should be the only one giving commands. Make sure every dog gets a chance to retrieve the ball!

Every infielder/owner should carry a ball. These can be used for "fake-out" throws. Some dogs will only retrieve a ball if their owner throws it, so after a ball is hit the owner can throw her ball in the direction that the actual ball was thrown.

The dogs whose team is at bat should be kept off the field. If you're playing on a baseball diamond, try keeping your dogs together in the fenced players' area. Alternatively, your team could appoint a dog-boy who is responsible for walking the dogs to the concession stand while your team hits.

At the Beach

The only people luckier than those who live by the beach are people who live by a beach that allows dogs!

A beach is a great place to spend time with your doggy: open spaces, sand to roll in, all the water in the world to swim in, and all kinds of doggies to meet, watch, and play with! Who could want more?

WHAT YOU'LL NEED:

- Bottled, cold water
- Umbrella or towel
- Dog swimming harness or flotation jacket (optional)
- Surfboard (optional)
- Sunscreen (for you!)

BEFORE YOU GO:

As much fun as the beach can be for you and your dog, it can also be very dangerous.

Beware of:

Undertow, riptides, and strong currents. If your doggy likes to swim, beware of the undertow, which can pull dogs underwater even in shallow water. Riptides and strong currents are also dangerous; they can carry even the strongest swimmer out too far. Keep a very close eye on Rufus as he swims to fetch the stick.

For extra protection, you might want to strap him into a swimming harness or flotation jacket.

Sun. The heat alone can be dangerous for Rufus, and all the running and playing he'll do on a warm day at the beach can cause him to get overheated much more quickly. Be sure to take plenty of fresh water for both of you, and, of course, provide him with shade (an umbrella, a propped up towel, a nearby bush) for rests in between the sprints and swims!

WHAT YOU'LL DO:

Now that you know what to look out for, it's time to have some fun!

Doggy Surfing. Many dogs love surfing as much as Frankie Avalon's pals. Take Rufus out with you on your board and see how he takes to it. There are no special doggy straps; Rufus will just stand on the board with you.

Burying You in the Sand. Train Rufus to "dig," and you can get him to bury you deep in the cool sand. This can get a little messy, so don't forget to cover your face with a bandana or hat.

In the Park

Much of our doggy's good life is spent at the park: all the grass she can eat, endless spots to roll in, lots of other dogs to play with—what's not to like? The park is also a great place for Bella to socialize, an activity that is vital to her health and happiness.

Most of the time we spend at the park is for our dog. We can let her run around, be free, and let her be herself—as long as she doesn't get into fights and stays within voice command. But the park is also a great place for practicing some of the games and tricks we've learned.

Here are a few suggested activities for the big doggy playground down the street:

Doggy Dubbing. This is an improvisational comedy technique that works best when a lot of dogs are around. You and other owners each pick a voice or an accent for your dog and make up dialogue between the dogs. A bassett hound could have a British accent. A shepherd could be German. A wolfhound could be Irish. A conversation could go like this:

"Achtung! That's my ball, klutz!"

"But me mates and me were goin' to play for a wee bit."

"Pardon me. I don't mean to be meddlesome, but I do believe that it's time for tea."

Trust us, it's hours of fun.

Doggy Stand-Up. If you fancy yourself a comedian, you've got a great audience at the park. Try out some of your jokes on the troops. They may not know what you're saying, but think of it this way: If you can play the park, you can play anywhere.

The Playground. A jungle gym—as long as there are no children around—can be a great place for you and Bella to have some fun. Lots of dogs like to run up the slide and then slip down. Some like to chase you back and forth on the swing. Most puppies enjoy a spin on the whirly-go-round. And everyone enjoys a good roll in the sand. The sky's the limit at the dog park playground.

In the Forest

Doggies love camping in the forest. With new soil to run around on and an endless array of trees marked only by strange and wild creatures, and smells unlike any at home, it's all a source of great fun.

For the most part, fun in the forest comes with the freedom of being in a new place. So nearly anything goes. The best strategy for having fun in the forest with Rufus is knowing what not to do.

Keep control. Always be aware of where Rufus is in the forest. If you're at your campsite, it's easy for him to get onto a rabbit's scent and take off in seconds. Keep him on a long leash at your campsite and within eyeshot on your hikes.

Watch the heat. When you're hiking with your pooch, always bring plenty of water and make sure you stop in the shade along the way.

Be aware of terrain. Rattlesnakes love to hide under rocks, a favorite place for dogs to sniff. A rattlesnake bite can be deadly, so keep Rufus under control. If the terrain is rocky, you may also want to make/invest in a set of doggy boots. Thick nylon soles (held on with elastic around the top) will help protect Rufus's feet from sharp rocks.

Beware of poisonous plants. Many plants, flowers, shrubs, trees, and fungi can be injurious to your beloved pooch. Familiarize yourself with some of the dangers indigenous to your area before you go out into the woods. The Resources section at the end of this book can be a good start, or call your vet to learn what to keep out of Rufus's mouth.

Always be careful, but have great doggy fun!

CHAPTER THREE

Indoors-y Days

Days spent indoors can be just as fun as outdoor ones—it's all in the way you choose to dog around. You can clean together or clean each other. You can read, watch TV, or practice your tricks. You can even test your doggy's psyche and tell your doggy's fortune.

In this chapter you'll learn how to make the best of a rainy day without getting doghouse fever.

Games

So you're rained in. Rufus isn't allowed outside due to a dramatic increase in the availability of mud. Before you settle down in front of the TV to watch Animal Planet together, try out some of our ideas.

Note: Watching TV is actually a fine indoor activity (see Movies to Watch, p. 60) as long as your doggy doesn't sit too close to the screen.

Cleaning Up the "Dog" House

The best way to describe this game is: "Clean your house and play with your dog at the same time." That's right—you'll end up with both a clean house and a tired dog. The object of the game is to get your dog to stop following you around the house while you're cleaning! This means that if you win you won't have to play very often. (But you probably will have to keep cleaning.)

WHAT YOU'LL NEED:

- A vacuum
- A broom and/or a mop
- A feather duster

WHAT YOU'LL DO:

Vacuum Attack. The vacuum attack is the first and primary move. Strategically, it's like leading with your best card. The bonus is that it weeds out the weak players early. As you vacuum, turn the tables on your dog and chase him around the house with your vacuum. If Rufus is not following you, feel free to get the game started by vacuuming directly underneath him. Warning: Vacuum attack is meant to *threaten* only. Do not under any circumstances suck any part of your dog into the vacuum.

Broom Maneuver. The broom maneuver is the second of a three-part series. The idea of this ploy is once again to turn the tables on your dog. As he follows you from the kitchen to the living room, turn around and start sweeping in front of him. Before every third sweep, tap the broom lightly on his rear end: Sweep-sweep-tap. Sweep-sweep-tap. This also works when mopping, but then the tap should be directed at his toes: Mop-mop-toes. Mop-mop-toes.

Feather Duster Harassment. This gambit is the final ploy. After stroking the feather duster across your tables and shelves, occasionally tap your dog on the tip of his nose and give a few flicks of the wrist, like it's a magic wand: Dust-dust-dangle. Dust-dust-dangle. If your dog sneezes, you are doing this move correctly.

Tips and Tricks:

The key to getting your dog to stop following you while you clean is to follow through. The feather duster maneuver is where you will have your greatest success. After you have mastered this move and your pooch has sneezed three times, try turning the duster on him directly. No matter what happens, don't let him get hold of your weapon!

You should be able to "dust him" into a corner or onto a couch. As the sneezing wears off and he comes back for more, hold up the duster before he gets too close. No dog in his right mind will come any closer—at least until next week.

Hide and Seek

To play an honest game of hide and seek with Rufus, he must be well versed in the "stay" and "come" commands. Otherwise, the game can quickly turn into "watch Mom yell at me, then try to climb under the bed." Which can be fun in its own right.

WHAT YOU'LL NEED:

- Hiding places
- Dog treats (optional)

WHAT YOU'LL DO:

The rules for Hide and Seek with your dog are the same as with humans. The only difference is that your dog is always It! Here's how you play:

1. **Give your dog a "sit" and "stay" command.**

2. **Go into another part of the house and hide.**

3. Once you're hidden, give your dog a "come" command.

Easy enough! A good game of Hide and Seek can bring hours of enjoyment to both you and your doggy.

Tips and Tricks:

There's always the possibility that your pooch can't find you if you only call him once and are really well hidden. If things are taking a while—and it seems like Rufus might have gone back to sleep—try calling him again. If a second call doesn't help, try making it to the couch before he finds you. A good bark can be translated as "ollie-ollie-oxen-free."

If neither of those methods works, try taking a treat with you to your hiding place. When your dog pokes his nose under the bed, give him a "Good boy!" and the treat.

Follow the Leader

Your dog looks to you as his leader (for the most part, at least). So a good game of Follow the Leader should come naturally.

It's also good practice for the doggy to follow your voice commands—"come," "this way," "down." If you need a little help, try taking a few treats along. And always remember, a pat on the head is worth two liver treats in the paw.

WHAT YOU'LL NEED:

- Your house

Note: Your floor plan may differ from ours, so use this as a guide.

1. Start in the living room. Walk around the coffee table and into the next room.

2. Crawl under the dining room table and into the kitchen.

3. Do some circles in the kitchen and walk into the den.

4. Climb over or under a low chair and go into the bedroom.

5. Climb onto the bed, under the sheets (if it's sheet-changing day), then go back to the living room.

Good Dog! Wasn't that fun?

Tips:

You can spice up your game of Follow the Leader a bit using some of these ploys.

1. Go in the opposite direction.

2. Set up an obstacle course of books or chairs if you have a small dog.

Indoor Tricks

Any day spent inside is a great day to teach your new dog old tricks (or vice versa). You have hours together inside to focus on one another and learn some tricks that you can take to the park on another day.

If you are unfamiliar with training your dog, revisit the Tricks section of the Outdoors-y Days chapter (p. 39) for some basic techniques.

Back Up. We love it when our doggy greets us joyfully at the front door, but not when she meets us on our way in from the grocery store with arms full of bags and a dog to trip over! Teach your dog to back up both when you are moving toward her with empty arms—try tossing a treat as you approach—and when your arms are full, and she'll catch on the next time you get back from a shopping trip.

Crawl. You never know when you and your dog may be trapped under a bleacher or running an obstacle course, but if you've taught her to crawl she'll be sure to succeed. Add a camouflage jacket (see Decorating T-Shirts, p. 20 or Doggy Painting, p. 15) and make Halloween that much more real! Start with your dog laying down, and slowly teach her to move forward on her belly, toward a treat.

Umbrella Fetch. A slight alteration of the newspaper fetch (see Tricks, p. 39), the umbrella fetch is perfect for a rainy day if you have to go out. This trick is an especially big hit after a dinner party. As one of your guests is leaving, Bella will be right there holding his umbrella (or someone's umbrella, anyway).

Movies

Everybody loves to sit down and watch the Westminster Dog Show with their dog, to watch his ears perk up when a like-bodied cousin prances across the screen. But what to do in the time between dog shows and walks in the park?

Why not rent a movie? Dogs have been in the movies for decades, and there's a lot to choose from in every genre. We have compiled a list of films for your dog and you to watch. Some are just for you, but others are best shared with your pooch.

Films for You

As Good as It Gets (1997)

A clever romantic comedy about an obsessive-compulsive man (played by Jack Nicholson, who won an Oscar for the role) and the dog who puts up with him.

Cujo (1983)

We debated whether this film was for you or your furry friend; we decided that it was too scary for your dog to watch. It's a classic horror film that suggests what might happen if you deny your pooch all the love in the world.

Doctor Dolittle (1967)

A great instructional comedy starring Rex Harrison, in which you'll learn all sort of tricks about caring for animals. There is also a 1998 version starring Eddie Murphy. Note Norm MacDonald's pivotal role as Lucky, the dog that changes Doctor Dolittle's outlook on life.

Ghostbusters (1984)

We like to watch this movie when we're upset with our dogs. Somehow thinking of them as Zuul and Vinz Clortho makes everything okay. Someone understands.

The Jerk (1979)

A brilliant Steve Martin comedy about a man whose foul-named dog stays with his master through the best and the worst of times.

Look Who's Talking Now (1993)

We recommend this film as an instructional video to help you understand what your dog is really trying to say.

There's Something about Mary (1998)

You'll laugh out loud when the little dog in this hilarious romp of a movie "gets his due"—and ends up in a full-body cast!

Films for Them

Beethoven (1992)
Beethoven's 2nd (1993)
Beethoven's 3rd (2000)
The *Beethoven* movies are sure to keep your dog's attention, unless—like the character Charles Grodin plays—your pup is disgusted by drool.

The Call of the Wild (1935)
A classic boy-and-his-dog story starring Clark Gable. We like to consider this one a basic for teaching dog morals.

Homeward Bound (1993)
Homeward Bound II: Lost in San Francisco (1996)
Great, uplifting films about the adventures of animals with voices of Michael J. Fox and Sally Field. Your dog will be impressed by the independence they show in a world without a master.

K-9 (1989)
A great buddy picture starring Jim Belushi and a German shepherd named Jerry Lee.

Lassie Come Home (1943)
A classic dog movie for you and for your best friend—full of loyalty, love, and the dog world at its purest. There is also a good 1994 version.

Oh, Heavenly Dog (1980)
Starring Chevy Chase and Benji, this movie is a classic detective spoof in which Chase dies and comes back in a dog's body.

Old Yeller (1957)
A Disney classic guaranteed to make the biggest tough guy and Doberman cry.

One Hundred and One Dalmatians (1961)
A great feel-good movie where good (the dogs) triumphs over evil (Cruella de Vil)! As a follow-up, get the 1996 live-action remake, *101 Dalmatians*, and its 2000 sequel, *102 Dalmations*, both starring Glenn Close.

The Shaggy Dog (1959)
The Shaggy D.A. (1976)
Two great Disney flicks in which a man turns into a sheepdog. In the first film he is woefully misunderstood—something any dog who's been unjustly punished will relate to! And what dog wouldn't want to see themselves as brilliant a detective as the Shaggy D.A.?

Turner & Hooch (1989)
A great buddy picture, starring Tom Hanks and the Arnold Schwarzenegger of the dog world! The Mastiff who plays Hooch is the key to solving the crime.

White Fang (1991)
This remake of the 1936 classic adventure of a boy and his dog, starring Ethan Hawke, is a sequel to *The Call of the Wild*.

Dog Tales: Story Time

There's no better way to spend down time than by reading about other dogs! Dogs in literature have been around for ages. Why, even Shakespeare loved to write about dogs.

A little doggy fiction will indeed bring both you and Bella closer together, because the more you understand her kind, the more you understand her. There are all kinds of doggy books to read, from fiction to nonfiction, from breed-specific to mutt training. But we like to focus on the doggy classics. These books about dogs stand the test of time.

The Call of the Wild and White Fang
by Jack London
Classic tales of dogs in the wild protecting their loved ones from the dangers that lurk there. Travel to Alaska and deep into the woods on an adventure.

Clifford the Big Red Dog
by Norman Bridwell
A great children's book series certain to pique your dog's interest when she sees the pictures of the largest red dog in the world!

Dog Heaven
by Cynthia Rylant
A great story to at least try to read to your pooch. This book really helps us realize that all good dogs do go to heaven.

Old Yeller
by Fred Gipson
A child and his dog. You may have seen the movie, but you haven't cried until you've read the book. Sure to help you appreciate every single day you have to spend with your dog.

Where the Red Fern Grows
by Wilson Rawls
Another child and his dog grow close chasing raccoons and a mountain lion, and then grow closer in death.

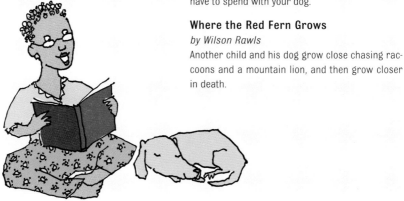

Standardized Tests for Your Dog

The Dog Personality Type Quiz

Take some time when you're not playing in the park to give your dog this personality quiz. It helps you understand your pooch's personality based on opposing behaviors: instinct vs. logic, fight vs. flight, habitual vs. spontaneous. This test might help you take another step toward understanding why Rufus barks every night at midnight.

1. **Your dog prefers:**
   - ☐ Sleeping
   - ☐ Hunting

2. **Your dog believes it is better to:**
   - ☐ Come when called
   - ☐ Pretend he doesn't hear anything

3. **When walking, your dog more often sees:**
   - ☐ His owner on the other end of the leash
   - ☐ That cat who was in the yard last week

4. **If your dog could speak, he would say:**
   - ☐ Hi, I missed you.
   - ☐ Did you know while you were gone I chased four birds, caught one mouse, and ate your shoe?

5. **When looking for a place to "do his business" your dog:**
   - ☐ Goes where he went yesterday
   - ☐ Sniffs for a clean spot until he finds one

6. **Playing with strange dogs:**
   - ☐ Makes your dog mad
   - ☐ Is more fun for your dog than rolling in garbage

7. **When your dog wants to go outside, he:**
   - ☐ Begs for you to open the front door
   - ☐ Uses the dog door

8. **Your dog believes it is better to:**
   - ☐ Be fed at the same time every day
   - ☐ Eat when he's hungry

9. **Your dog is more attracted to:**
   - ☐ The sidewalk
   - ☐ The grass

10. **When that guy in the blue uniform comes and puts papers in that box by the front door, your dog is:**
    - ☐ Excited
    - ☐ Pissed

11. **Your dog barks:**
    - ☐ When barked at
    - ☐ Whenever he darn well pleases

12. **Your dog is more comfortable:**
    - ☐ Directly under your feet
    - ☐ On the couch by the window

13. **At a river or lake, your dog:**
    - ☐ Gets a cool, refreshing drink
    - ☐ Swims after the ducks

14. **When your dog gets a new chew toy, he:**
    - ☐ Buries it for a rainy day
    - ☐ Eats a hole through it

15. **Your dog believes that children:**
    - ☐ Take attention away from him
    - ☐ Are fun to lick

16. In the morning, your dog gets up:

☐ When you do

☐ When the newspaper delivery boy is two houses away

17. When marking territory, your dog believes in:

☐ Marking everything in sight

☐ Staying close to home

18. When there's a knock at the door, your dog:

☐ Waits to see who comes in

☐ Runs to get dibs on "first licks"

19. When your dog hears, "Who wants a treat?" he thinks:

☐ "Roll over, get a treat. Roll over, get a treat. Roll over, get a treat."

☐ "Great, I've got to roll over again."

20. At a dinner party, your dog:

☐ Waits under the table for something to fall off

☐ Puts his chin on a stranger's lap and gives his best "puppy eyes"

SCORING

Give your dog one point for each first answer and two points for every second answer, and a treat for just being a dog.

20–26: You love your master. You love your life as a dog. What could be better? You do as you're told, when you're told. You don't like change at all.

27–33: You like your life as a dog, but you think there could be more. If only you could figure out how to speak English. You've got great ideas for places to go, people to see, but you just don't know how to drive.

34–40: You are a banshee. Completely independent. You love the world, and it is your piece of bacon. You can't understand who these people are who yell at you all the time. They live in your house, and you can't figure out how to get them to leave for more than eight hours a day.

The Dog Aptitude Test

Another fun test to do with your dog indoors is the Dog Aptitude Test. You can try this at home or even at the pet store when looking for a new "best friend." These challenges are designed to help you determine your doggy's general personality, but don't expect your dog to fit exactly into any of the categories below. Remember, no one type is better than another. And your personality comes into play as well, of course.

KEY:

MBF—Man's (and Woman's) Best Friend. This pooch loves you and everything you do. He is a dog's dog.

MGF—Man's (and Woman's) Good Friend. This pooch loves you and himself. With some training he will do almost everything you say. Unless, of course, he feels very strongly about it.

MPGF—Man's (and Woman's) Pretty Good Friend. This pooch likes you and loves himself. He may master the basics, such as "sit," "stay," and "come," but the rest will probably take some work. He is very independent and strong willed. On the plus side, his spirit may bring you hours of amusing anecdotes.

1. The "Get It" Test

Find a toy that truly entices your dog. If you're not sure which one does the trick, try holding up several different ones to get his attention. Whichever one he lunges for is the right item. Roll or toss the toy at least six feet away from the dog and watch his response.

MBF—runs straight to the toy and attacks it with joy, showing you his prize.

MGF—runs to the toy, but he may bat it around and play with it a bit. His enthusiasm is more about curiosity.

MPGF—ignores both the toy and you.

2. The "Bring It" Test

Throw the toy again, then call your pooch by name. See if he brings the toy back to you.

MBF—runs back to you and drops the toy at your feet.

MGF—comes back to you but leaves the toy, or comes back to you with the toy but won't give it up without a little play first.

MPGF—ignores both the toy and you.

3. The "Find It" Test

Reclaim the toy and place it between your legs, under a piece of furniture, or in another appropriate hiding place. Make sure the toy is still slightly in sight of the dog.

MBF—becomes excited and attentive to you and the toy. He may search, dig, or whine for it and your affections.

MGF—stares at you wondering when you'll pull that fun toy out from its hiding place and throw it again.

MPGF—ignores both the toy and you.

4. The "Play with It" Test

With the toy firmly in your grasp, entice the pooch to take the toy with his mouth.

MBF—snatches the toy and fights you for it . . . all in the name of fun, of course.

MGF—tries for the toy but doesn't hang on for too long.

MPGF—ignores both the toy and you.

5. The "Own It" Test

Most dogs will want to keep their prize once they have it, so this test allows you to judge whether it is the toy or your approval that the dog wants. During the "Play with It" Test, release or drop the toy at your dog's feet.

MBF—encourages you to pick up the toy and play with it again.

MGF—takes his prize and buries it somewhere. He may ask you to play with his belly instead.

MPGF—ignores both the toy and you.

6. The "Follow It" Test

Have a partner hold the dog while you visibly shake the toy from across the room.

MBF—runs immediately and excitedly to—or into—you.

MGF—takes his time to get to you. When he gets there, he's more interested in you scratching his belly than in that toy.

MPGF—ignores both the toy and you.

7. The "Focus It" Test

The "Focus It" Test helps you to know who is really in charge. Hold the toy out to the dog until you have his attention. When he looks at you, maintain eye contact with him for at least twenty seconds.

MBF—looks at you for a short time, but then looks away so as not to challenge your Alpha-ness.

MGF—looks at you and does not look away—or won't make eye contact with you.

MPGF—ignores you.

Relaxing with Your Dog

After all the games and tricks and tests and treats, you and your pooch may be plumb doggied out. That's when we can take a lesson from our dogs and lay down for a nap. Dream about chasing rabbits. Stare out the window at the cars passing by. It is a dog's life when it comes to relaxing with your dog.

For a more organized relaxation, take a look at the Meditation section (p. 83). These techniques are good for when you just want to kick up your paws and take a load off.

Sleep on their level. If you lay down on the floor with Bella, she'll love you for it. How often does she get to be so close to you? You can both do some good snuggling on the floor in any of these sleeping positions:

Spoons. Curl up around your pooch, with your belly to her back.

Doggy pillow. Put your head on Bella's rear end and use her as a pillow.

Human pillow. Put Bella's head on your rear and let her use you as a pillow.

Back to back. Put your back against Bella's and feel the security of having dog's eyes in the back of your head.

Watch out the window. Your dog spends hours staring out the front window watching the cats, cars, and walkers stroll by. Join her, and find hours of enjoyment. Tip: Don't forget to run outside and jump at the gate when the mailman comes!

Animal TV. Always a good fallback. Cable channels run animal shows all the time, and it's easy to get your pooch hooked on any one of them.

Paw Reading and
Doggy Fortune-Telling

We can learn a lot about our dogs by reading the messages that are ingrained in their very being. The paw holds the key to the doggy past and future. We've mapped out the basic shapes and lines on a paw and compiled an easy-to-use translator to help you read your dog's paw.

This is a great activity for birthday parties (see p. 118) or if you're just sitting at home and Rufus seems curious about his future.

WHAT YOU'LL NEED:

- Paper
- Children's bath paint
- A bowl
- Your dog's paw

WHAT YOU'LL DO:

It is easier to read your dog's paw if you get a paw print on a piece of paper first. Just dip his pad in a bowl of watered-down children's bath paint (see Doggy Painting, p. 15), and press his foot onto a clean sheet of paper. You may have to do this several different times before you get a clear print.

Match the shapes below to the shapes on your dog's paw.

Compare the color of the shapes and lines to the color of the paw when clean. If they are darker or lighter, make a note of that. This information is essential for an accurate paw reading. Also note any breaks or inconsistencies in the continuity of a shape or line.

Now form a simple sentence using your notes; for example, "The heart pad is broken and black."

Using the descriptions below, interpret the shapes and lines; for example, "Rufus's love life is no longer and it is forgotten." Translation: Rufus has been neutered.

See how easy it is?

Paw Shapes and Lines:

Heart Pad—reflects your dog's heart. Primarily represents the importance of his emotional and physical relationships to dogs and humans. A wide pad indicates a big heart.

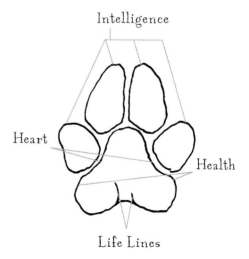

Intelligence

Heart

Health

Life Lines

Life Lines—reflect the strength of your dog's spirit. A long lifeline means a long life.

Intelligence Pads—reflects your dog's cognitive abilities, his capacity to listen and learn, or lack thereof. A long, more oval pad shows a smart and independent dog. A short, round pad reflects that he's not the sharpest knife in the drawer.

Health Line—reflects the future of your dog's vet visits. If the line is not present, you have a healthy dog! If the line is present, and has numerous breaks in it, you might want to think about a trip to the vet.

Colors

(to read accurate colors, examine your dog's paw directly—without paint on it!):

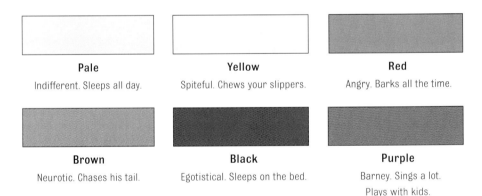

Pale	**Yellow**	**Red**
Indifferent. Sleeps all day.	Spiteful. Chews your slippers.	Angry. Barks all the time.
Brown	**Black**	**Purple**
Neurotic. Chases his tail.	Egotistical. Sleeps on the bed.	Barney. Sings a lot. Plays with kids.

Travel Days

Whether you live with Rufus Kerouac or Bella Earhart, doggy travel is always an adventure! One of the best ways to spend time with your pooch is to travel with her. Doggy travel generally takes a little extra work and preparation. You should always "handle with care."

Take extra care to check on your doggy's health before taking any extended trips or vacations together. Also, it's a good idea to have a set routine—eating, sleeping, going to the bathroom, and so forth—before traveling. Try to maintain your dog's regular schedule as much as possible.

Even trips that aren't for fun require special preparation and care—especially if you're going to the V-E-T! In this chapter, you'll learn how to handle all sorts of trips, from vacations and moving to vet visits.

Road Trips

It's a good idea to prepare a few weeks in advance for an extended road trip with your dog. Make sure that she can deal with travel. Most dogs can handle a quick jaunt to the park or to the trails for a hike, but being in the car for several hours at a time without returning to familiar territory is a different challenge. Try building up to long trips with some short overnight travel.

Make sure that your dog is in good health. A call or visit to the vet will confirm that Bella is up to date on her shots, properly tagged and identifiable, and fit for the road.

Check ahead for dog-friendly hotels and restaurants (see Resources, p. 122). Many cities offer an assortment of dog-friendly activities. A little research can go a long way toward comfort for both of you during the trip.

Be prepared for different environments. If Bella lives in California and is driving with you to the cold winter mountains of Colorado, she has to adjust as much as you do. If you're going to the desert, bring more water than she usually drinks and a first aid kit for snakebites. Be aware that just because she doesn't suffer from fleas in your hometown doesn't mean that your vacation spot will be free of them. Also bring familiar objects from home, like a blanket or chew toy, to remind your dog that not everything is different.

When You're on the Road:

1. Never leave your dog in a hot car!!! On warm days, the time it takes for you to run into the store is all it takes for your car's temperature to reach fatal levels. Don't risk it. Tie her up to a tree outside; she'll enjoy that so much more anyway.

2. Drive with a window cracked. A good breeze is essential for a fun and healthy doggy car ride. Don't open the window far enough that Bella could jump out, though—just enough so she can feel the breeze on her face.

3. Use that doggy seatbelt. Seatbelts or harnesses for your dog, found in pet supply stores, are highly recommended. And don't forget to put yours on, too.

4. Bring plenty of food and water. Some folks go as far as bringing bottled water from home, claiming water that's not from the home tap makes their dog sick. Some also feed their dog less on road trips to avoid car sickness. Other folks let their dog choose how much to eat and drink.

Good! Now you're ready to travel with your pooch. Have fun! You'll probably find that something John Steinbeck said is especially true with a dog: "We don't take trips, trips takes us!"

Essential Doggy Sights to See

There are some great places around America for you and Bella to visit. As you hit the road, plan to make a few stops along the way. Just think of the joy Bella will get when you surprise her with some just-for-doggy visits! And don't forget to capture the travel moments on camera to add to your journal/scrapbook.

The East

Madison Square Garden—Pennsylvania Plaza on 7th Avenue, between 31st and 33rd Streets, New York, New York. Home to the Westminster Kennel Club Championships! For Bella, a stop by Madison Square Garden is like a stop by Yankee Stadium after the World Series. Hint: The championships are held in mid-February, so if you go toward the end of the month there should be plenty of leftover dog smells.

Dog Town—There's a Dog Town in both Washington County, Maine, and Armstrong County, Pennsylvania. Go visit because everyone likes to see places that are named after them!

The South and the Midwest

The World's Largest Fire Hydrant—At the State Fire Museum of Texas, Beaumont, Texas. Oh the sheer joy! A fire hydrant that stands twenty-four feet tall. A dog could

spend all day marking points along the circumference and never get bored. Disney studios built the hydrant to celebrate the rerelease of its animated video *One Hundred and One Dalmatians*.

Dog Town, Alabama—Located in DeKalb County. This town's not big enough for the two of our dogs!

The West

Lake Chelan, Washington—Lake Chelan is the location for the classic dog movie *Lassie Come Home*. You and Bella can run through the doggy-field equivalent of the Alps in *The Sound of Music*, or practice calling her over the hill. "Bella! Come home!"

The Largest Trees in the World: Redwood National Park, Northwestern California—The Redwood Forest houses the largest and oldest trees in the country. Unfortunately, the trees must remain the stuff of your doggy's dreams—dogs aren't allowed in the forest itself. There are some leashed and unleashed areas around the park, though.

Dog Town, California—Yup. There's one here, too, in Northern California. It's north of San Francisco on Route 1. As an added bonus, while you're in those parts, you can go to Yorkville, California. The Martz Winery houses the "World's Largest Winery Cat." They say his name is Corky and he loves chicken.

Making the Ride to the Vet Fun

Nobody likes to go to the doctor, especially your doggy. Think of it from her perspective. First, she starts on a walk or a drive. This could mean a day at the park! A hike in the mountains! Maybe she's hoping to go wherever it is you leave for every day at eight and return home from smelling of at five.

But then she's thrown a curve ball. That building. The VET! The place that smells like every other cat and dog in the world, plus some things she's never even seen before. The place that every dog on this side of the tracks has marked as his own. The place where they say she's "cute, but fat" and has to go on a diet. Then a strange lady in a white coat steps into the small, windowless room, feeds her a liver treat, talks all nicety-nice, and then sticks her with a needle. All this and a thermometer up the rear, too. Who wouldn't hate the vet?

Most dogs are sharp enough to recognize when they get close to the vet's office and many times anxiety can set in. We've devised several techniques for making the trip to the vet fun and distracting enough that the actual doctor's office visit will be a walk in the park.

WHAT YOU'LL NEED:

- A spare hour before the appointment

WHAT YOU'LL DO:

Make the journey your destination. Here are some suggestions as to how:

Head to the park. It is a really good idea, depending on how serious your trip to the vet is, to spend as much time in the park beforehand as possible. The longer your doggy has to be at the vet, the longer you two should be in the park. Let her run and be free, and give her a chance to do her "business." This will help reduce anxiety once she figures out where you're really going.

Roll down a window (if you're in the car)**.** This is a must for every car trip, especially ones with such a disappointing destination.

Take a different route. Your dog knows where she's going, usually about a block or two before you get to the doc. Mix it up a little. Find a scenic route.

Distraction, distraction, distraction. It's a good idea to talk to your pet during the entire trip to the vet. A simple repetition of questions keeps her on her toes and looking out for anything but the vet. "Where's the kitty? Where's the baby? Where's the puppy?"

Sing. A rousing rendition of "How Much Is That Doggy in the Window" is bound to lift her spirits. Also, the bond you create will let her know that you're not only that evil-person-who-takes-her-to-get-her-temperature-taken.

AFTER THE VISIT:

Remember how your parents would reward you for not having any cavities by taking you to get a soda and a donut? Didn't it make the dentist bearable? So why not take your doggy by the pet store for a pig's ear or some fake bacon? Nothing says lovin' after a trip to the vet like a rawhide muffin.

Then, of course, depending on the severity of treatment during your doggy's visit, there's always the drive-thru cheeseburger. But you didn't hear that from us!

Moving to a New House

When moving to a new house, almost all dogs suffer some form of anxiety, which can last anywhere from an hour to several weeks. Some dogs even have trouble if furniture gets rearranged; they'll circle the "disturbed" area, displaying their awareness that something is off. There are stories of dogs traveling vast distances to return to familiar territory. But since you want to keep your dog close by, here are a few tips for moving:

1. Plan to spend at least two days with your dog when you get to a new home. You are the leader of the pack and also the most familiar thing to your dog. The more time you can spend consoling and comforting and familiarizing him with his new home, the better.

2. Before you move, establish a special area for your dog. This could be a blanket, couch, or bed that will be his comfort zone, no matter where you go. Take a blanket or pillow from his zone with you when you take short trips in the car. It will reassure your dog that his comfort zone will always be there.

3. If you will be traveling by plane, consult one of the resources (see page 122) for advice on cargo versus cabin travel. Some dogs love to fly, but others wouldn't do it for all the shoes in the world. Many airlines allow small dogs to travel in your carry-on bag if it fits under your seat. Call first or check with your travel agent before buying your ticket.

4. When you arrive at your new home, take several short walks with your dog each day. Don't go too far at first. Let him smell and mark and become familiar with his new territory. Go in different directions until your dog gets the lay of the land.

Many dogs experience anxiety attacks so severe that they vomit or go to the bathroom in the new house or yard. Be patient: this too shall pass. If it persists for more than a few days, however, call your new vet.

Healthy Days

Maintaining a healthy doggy mind and doggy body are key to your doggy's well-being. A healthy pooch is a happy pooch. A happy pooch is a well-balanced pooch. A well-balanced pooch does whatever you say (or so we hope).

In this chapter you will learn how to reach a higher level of doggy understanding through meditation and yoga. You'll also learn how to treat your canine pals in case of an emergency. Overall, you'll learn how to make the most of your dog's life.

Self-Esteem and Mental Health

It's a fact: Most dogs feel, look, and act better when they have something to do. The key to a happy dog is proper care, routine, and activity.

Even if you only have time to pet Bella for thirty minutes a day, she will still expect and look forward to this time every day. And yes, dogs can tell time. Dinnertime, walk time, play time, and bedtime!

Keeping your dog occupied may not pose a problem if she has a wide open space to play in, but this can be a greater challenge if you live in an urban area. Either way, we suggest starting simply.

Take ten to thirty minutes each day to teach her tricks and obedience. Even a "game" of "sit" and "stay" will stimulate her mind.

If your dog is well socialized and follows commands, find an animal agency that trains dogs to visit hospitals, nursing homes, or home-bound residences. They will give Bella a series of tests. The simplest will involve simple voice commands like "sit" and "stay." More complicated stress tests will place Bella in a room of wheelchairs and people to gauge how calm she remains. They may also have many people petting her at the same time to see how she reacts.

If Bella doesn't pass the agency's test the first time, go home and work on her weak points. Most organizations will let you try out as many times as you want.

Once your dog is happy, she's ready to make others happy, too. Therapy dogs love going to work because it means giving all kinds of love and getting lots of petting.

Any stimulation you can offer routinely will open your dog's mind and help her attitude, health, and esteem. Whether it's visiting hospitals, the office, or fetching the paper, give your dog tasks and her happiness will shine.

Meditation

Be here now. Your dog is ever present, and you can learn a lot by meditating with him. No, we're not talking about sitting on a hardwood floor together chanting, "Bone. Bone." (Although it is fun to say.) You can practice several different kinds of meditation with your dog.

These techniques are for beginners, because if you're a Buddhist then you're already one with your dog. Your first session should last no more than ten minutes. Depending on how Rufus responds, start adding time. Rufus will make it clear when he's had enough.

Sitting Meditation

The cool grass. A silent breeze. The sunset. And your doggy under one arm.

Sitting meditation with your dog is not difficult. Pet your dog gently and evenly from head to back as the two of you sit quietly, facing the world.

Breathe in through your nose and out through your mouth, concentrating on the rhythm of Rufus's panting.

See what your dog sees. The grass, the trees, the sky . . . the mailman across the street. As you take in what is in front of you, consider that the present moment is the only moment.

Be the Dog. Rufus is not thinking

about that cat that got away this morning. Or the gas man who jumped the fence after reading the meter. He is only where he is. Sitting in the park with his best friend. Follow his lead on this one.

Walking Meditation

For eons, monks have practiced walking meditation—so why not try it on your daily jaunts with Bella? The principles are the same, but you must know in your mind that you are not controlling the walk.

Unless Bella is very well trained and will heel (walk by your side at your pace), she should be on a "free-leash." A "free-leash," while still controlled by you, gives her the opportunity to determine the course of the walk. Follow these steps to a fulfilling and spiritual walk with your doggy.

Go with the flow. With each step, let your dog take you. This may mean that you need to stop at every single tree. Look under every single car. Smell every single piece of trash. Just let it be. Do what she does.

Think quality, not quantity. If you are "with" your dog, letting her lead you, then two or three streets of concentrated sniffing and stopping are better than six or seven with the two of you tugging at each other.

Note: Cats are as distracting and unnerving to dogs as thoughts of the past or future are to humans. Even one suggestive scent of them has the uncanny ability to pull a dog out of its state of mind. If your dog smells or sees a cat, stop. As Bella barks and growls and tugs, stay still. Examine your own thoughts of the future or the past. Observe them and then let them go. Your dog will eventually do the same. Like your thoughts, cats will always be there; there is no harm in letting them go until they manifest themselves.

Dog Yoga: Doga

If you've practiced yoga before, then you're probably familiar with the movements called "Upward Dog" and "Downward Dog." You're also probably familiar with the way that yoga can balance your mind and your body.

It can do the same for our dogs. After a few twenty-minute sessions of doga we find them more centered and relaxed—even asleep. (Not that they need our help sleeping!)

Warning: For the first few doga sessions, move slowly. Give Bella a chance to get used to being moved by you. If she doesn't like what you're doing, she'll let you know, and you should stop. With older dogs, we recommend that you make smaller movements with their limbs. If you feel any resistance, stop.

WHAT YOU'LL NEED:

- The floor (or a bed if you allow Bella on your bed)
- Relaxing music (think running water or wind blowing through treetops)

WHAT YOU'LL DO:

Before starting Doga, take a few minutes to let Bella become present by performing Sitting Meditation (p. 83).

All moves are performed with your dog laying on her side. Complete one full side before rolling her over and repeating the same exercises.

Beginners to doga should practice with their dog lying down. As dog and owner become more comfortable with the moves, you may try them with your dog standing.

Lay Bella on her side and work her hind leg:

Ballet Dancer

1. With one hand under her thigh and the other under her knee, stretch her leg slowly forward in a straight line toward her front limb. Hold for a count of five.

2. Using the same hold, stretch her leg straight back toward her tail. Hold for a count of five.

3. Repeat five to ten times.

Ham Bone/Chicken Bone

1. From the Ballet Dancer position, pull your dog's leg upward. Rotate her leg (bent at the knee is fine) clockwise in five complete circles. The movement should come from her hip. The movement should look like she's riding a bicycle, if she could do that.

2. Move the leg in counterclockwise circles. If your dog's leg feels like a chicken wing, then you're doing the move correctly.

3. Do not force this move. If your dog resists, continue on to a new move. Otherwise, repeat five to ten times.

Running in Place

1. This move should be slow and even: With one hand above the knee and one below, bend your dog's leg from the knee until she won't let you go any further. Hold for a count of five.

2. Using the same hold, straighten your dog's leg from the knee. Hold for a count of five. This only moves the knee, as if she were running in slow motion.

3. Repeat five to ten times.

Achilles Dog

1. Being careful to move slowly and evenly, place one hand above the hind leg's ankle and one hand below.

2. Bend your dog's foot up toward her belly until you feel resistance. Hold for a count of five.

3. Using the same hold, bend the foot down. Hold for a count of five. Older dogs have less flexibility in their feet than younger dogs, so do not be surprised if the foot of your two-year-old puppy can bend twice as far as that of your eight-year-old dog.

4. Repeat five to ten times.

Move on to the forelegs:

Doggy Paddle

1. This move is similar to Ballet Dancer: With one hand around her upper foreleg and the other on her elbow, stretch her foreleg toward her head in a straight line. Hold for a count of five.

2. Using the same hold, stretch her foreleg back toward her tail. Hold for a count of five.

3. Repeat five to ten times.

Bicep Flex

1. Similar to Running in Place: With one hand above your dog's elbow and the other below, bend her foreleg forward. Hold for a count of five.

2. Using the same hold, straighten out her foreleg. Hold for a count of five.

3. Repeat five to ten times.

Hello-Goodbye

1. Similar to Achilles Dog: With one hand above your dog's wrist and one hand below, bend her wrist forward. Hold for a count of five.

2. Using the same hold, straighten her paw. Hold for a count of five. If it looks like your dog is waving, you're doing it right.

3. Repeat five to ten times.

   Once you've completed all the moves on one side, roll Bella over and repeat.

Tips and Tricks:

As an extra doga move, bend and straighten your dog's toes and fingers at the end of each move. Some dogs do not like this at all; others would let you do it all day.

Doggy Massage

This is a movement in the doggy care world that is gaining quite a bit of approval today. After all, every doggy likes a good rub down. And if you're going to spend some time petting Rufus, why not give him a true massage?

WHAT YOU'LL NEED:

- The floor (or a bed—if you allow Rufus on your bed)
- Relaxing music (see Doga)

WHAT YOU'LL DO:

Doggy massage is a bit different from your treatments at the spa, where you go to relax. When your doggy goes to your home spa, well, it's up to him whether he'll relax or not.

Most dogs love the attention. After a session or two, Rufus may start to rely on a good rub after a long day of bird chasing to work those knots out of his body. Give it a shot! Not only will he love you for it, you'll also get to know his body and become aware of any physical changes in it.

1. Lay your dog on his side. If you're going to work a specific area of his body, be sure that area faces up.

2. With both hands flat, stroke from his paw to his heart. This gets the mojo flowing.

3. Starting at his rear end, do five repetitions of good solid rubbing, working your way down to his paw. Your dog will let you know if you're doing it too hard.

4. Gently work your way up your dog's back muscles. Hint: If you feel a twitch, that means the muscle is tense and tired. Give that area a little extra gentle attention.

5. Work your dog's shoulders and front limbs. A gentle but firm kneading motion with both hands often sends him into ecstasy.

6. Rub your dog's head and neck, working the doggy tension away from the heart. Hint: Some dogs really like to have their ears rubbed, and they can be like acupressure points.

7. Repeat on his other side.

If Rufus hasn't become completely disinterested at this point, give him a good overall sweep. From his feet back toward his heart and from his head to his heart, pet and stroke him rapidly to get the blood flowing.

Tips and Tricks:

Don't be surprised if Rufus looks at you funny the first time you try doggy massage. But assure him with treats or words that if he tries it he'll like it.

Most dogs do get anxious after lying prone for five or ten minutes. If Rufus tries to get up, gently push his head back down. This may buy you another five or ten minutes. He'll love you for it! (Well, he'll love you anyway but he'll feel great after a massage.)

Aromatherapy

The smells that interest dogs tend to repulse people. But since dogs communicate through smells, it is fun to expose them to new ones.

There are several smells that you can try to get you started. Your dog may get a little spastic, but he will certainly be stimulated! You can either create these smells, or just stop at the door when you come home and let your dog sniff some new odors.

Below you will find a list of smells, followed by the canine reaction to each one.

Bacon:
Cooked, sweet, greasy bacon!

Puppy:
Who's that? Where is she? Let me at her!

Shoes:
Where have you been today? Oh, that place.

Roast Turkey:
Cooked, sweet, roasted turkey!

Kitty:
Oh, evil kitty!

Hydrant:
Wait! This is my hydrant!

Haircuts

It's so easy to go to the groomer, drop off Rufus, and return eight hours later to find a sweet-smelling, shaved, and happy semblance of the wreck you brought in just hours earlier. Most groomers even send him home with a bow tied onto his collar.

But what's the fun in that? You and your dog can bond and save some money with some simple at-home grooming. Just like when mom used to come at you with a pair of scissors, mumbling, "How can you see?"

Doggy haircuts can be tricky. It all depends on the dog. The easygoing dog will simply love the attention: the touching, the petting, the buzz of the razor. You could shave his name into his back and he'd be happy. A terrified dog hates the razor. Cutting his hair is easy, because as soon as you grab his collar and fire up that razor, he gets so nervous he couldn't move if he wanted to. Then there's the difficult dog. He becomes Cujo the second you start even cleaning the razor. He's a tough one, but with a little love and training you can still win him over. But we'll get to those techniques in a minute.

Vets and dog owners alike tend to disagree on how long your dog's hair should be. Some dog owners like to shave their longhaired dogs all the time. In the summer, they say, "It's too hot." And in the winter they say, "They get too dirty."

Believe it or not, some vets say that dogs that are naturally longhaired stay cooler in the summer with their full coat. This has been disputed by owners (mainly because your vet doesn't have to vacuum up ten pounds of shed Husky-hairball from under your couch every weekend).

So, to suit dog owners and vets alike, below you'll find directions for several different types of mutt cuts.

WHAT YOU'LL NEED:

- Electric shears (about $100— roughly as much as to two trips to the groomers)
- Hair clips
- A helper (if possible)
- Treats

- Brushes:
  - ▸ Thin-toothed for short hair
  - ▸ Medium-toothed for medium-length hair
  - ▸ Full-bristle for long, thick hair

BEFORE YOU START:

If you are going to cut near and around your dog's head, ears, eyes, or mouth we recommend that you have either a helper or a lot of experience. We suggest that you only trim around the dog's ears with the shears. It's easier and it makes for a nice Prince Valiant look.

WHAT YOU'LL DO:

The "Buzz." Clearly the simplest cut, both to perform and to maintain. The tightest buzz can be achieved by running the shears upward against the growth of your dog's coat. This technique is very close and even.

The "High and Tight." Really more of a medium trim. Run the shears down your dog's coat to create a short-on-the-sides but long-on-the-top effect. This cut may take a little more time, because every dog's coat has a different thickness and it takes longer to get all of it to the same length. Try using an adapter or a comb on your shears. Many are made to clip right on, and they come in multiple lengths.

The "Doggy Mullet." Created by using the buzz technique on your dog's back between his shoulder blades. The mullet works best on longhaired dogs because his side and leg hair should all be left long.

The "Doggy Reverse Mullet." Achieved by using the buzz technique between the undersides of your dog's shoulders. This includes a close shave of his belly and legs. Use hair clips and brushes to hold a long-haired dog's coat out of the way. Some folks argue that this cut keeps a dog cool in the summer because the direct contact with the cool grass helps lower body temperature.

Tips and Tricks:

For those of you who are the masters of a difficult dog—you know, the dog who won't clean his room, take a bath, eat all of his dinner, or sit still for a haircut—there are a few tricks you can try.

Introduce your dog to the clippers. Start simply by leaving the clippers out on the floor for a half an hour or so, so your dog can sniff at them. The next day, while you're watching TV, turn the clippers on and off several times, letting them run for a few minutes each time. This will help Rufus get used to the sound.

Start small. When you finally get your dog subdued enough to sit for a haircut, try one of the quicker haircuts (the Mullet or Reverse Mullet).

Use treats. Serve them for every step of the process.

When all else fails: Get a friend to hold him down—obviously, not too roughly. But some dogs do just have to be muscled through a haircut.

Bath Time

If you fall into the "not so rich and famous" category, then you probably aren't planning on building your dog a special bathroom equipped with a custom dog tub and drying kennel. So you need the obvious yet effective solution to bath time: Bathe the really stinky ones where you bathe.

Bathing small dogs, like toy breeds, is an easy problem to solve. Your kitchen sink with a built-in sprayer will save you $40 at the groomers. But be sure to put a trap in the drain to catch all that dog hair. She is easily dried afterward with your blow-dryer, but be careful that you don't burn her.

A 150-pound Newfoundland, however, is a different story. In the summer there's a simple solution: Take her outside and turn on the hose. But the colder months offer a greater challenge.

You can spend $10 to $15 at a do-it-yourself dog wash (check your local newspaper). But if you're cheap (like us!), you and a partner—one of you must be stronger than your dog—can finagle her into the tub and scrub away.

WHAT YOU'LL NEED:

- Bathtub
- Dog shampoo
- Dog conditioner
- Blow-dryer (in colder months)
- Towels

WHAT YOU'LL DO:

1. Get the dog into the tub. Do whatever you have to. A good way to pick up your dog is with one arm underneath her belly and one arm underneath her chest. Hold firmly and lift.

2. Test the water temperature. Use cool to lukewarm water.

3. Wet, lather, rinse, condition, and rinse. When rinsing out the shampoo, don't worry about every last sud. You're just going to condition afterward, so wait for the final spray-off to be thorough.

4. We find that hundreds of cupfuls of water work just as well as one spray-down with a shower attachment. Most pet stores also sell a shower attachment fixture that fits over your faucet and extends over your dog.

5. Dry her off in the tub. If you use a blow-dryer, keep your hand against your dog's skin as a heat gauge. If you use towels, dry your dog as thoroughly as you can before removing her from the tub.

Tips and Tricks:

Cotton in your dog's ears and Vaseline above her eyelids help keep water out of these delicate parts.

A towel over her back, when you take her out of the tub, will help control where the water goes when she decides it's time to shake.

A little doggy cologne makes her that much sweeter.

Of course, a treat after such an ordeal is necessary—for the dog and for you!

Cooking for Your Dog

Even though veterinarians recommend that a dog's diet remain consistent and steady (meaning you shouldn't change the dog food frequently), occasional treats are always welcome! Surely eating the same lamb and rice clumps day in and day out gets somewhat monotonous.

We are all inclined to give our beloved pets a little variety once in a while: a nibble of pork chop fat, a bite of breakfast bacon. The way to our dog's heart is through his snout, so to truly win over your dog, make a special treat with your own two hands that's just to his liking.

Appetizers

The Ever Popular "Bone"

It might be easier just to buy a bag of dog bones at your local pet store or supermarket, but to prepare a "bone" from scratch is the highest form of love. In the same amount of time as you would spend reading the labels of store-bought products, trying to figure out what sodium bisulfate is (and if it's really something you want to give to your pet), you could have cooked a full batch of homemade bones.

Note: These treats can be used for special rewards (bringing your slippers or newspaper), but we recommend a limited distribution. (Unless, of course, you're prepared to hear the vet tell you how overweight your dog is.)

WHAT YOU'LL NEED:

- ¹/₂–1 pound raw ground turkey
- ¹/₄ cup chicken broth
- ¹/₃ cup mashed potatoes
- ¹/₃ cup cottage cheese
- 1 teaspoon smooth peanut butter

Prep. time: 10 minutes

Cooking time: 45 minutes

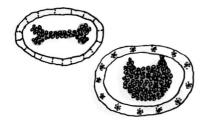

WHAT YOU'LL DO

1. Preheat the oven to 375°.

2. In a large bowl, mix all ingredients together.

3. Mold the mixture into small shapes (bones, cats, newspapers, or mail-men) or roll it out with a rolling pin and cut it into shapes with a cookie cutter, placing the pieces on an ungreased cookie sheet.

4. Bake for 45 minutes. Let cool thoroughly before tossing one to your pooch.

Makes ¹/₂ to 1 dozen "good dog" appetizers.

"Oh How I Love My Liver" Treats

This recipe is a version of the treat that your vet probably uses before giving Rufus a shot or taking some blood. They can be a valuable asset to you, and a time-honored appetizer for your dog.

Note: These treats can be used as rewards for tricks, obedience, or just general "good-dogginess." But be warned: Liver treats are the potato chips of the doggy world—no dog is content to eat just one.

WHAT YOU'LL NEED:

- 1 package chicken livers
  (approximately 24)

Prep. time: 5 minutes
Cooking time: 45 minutes,
plus 24 hours to dry out thoroughly

WHAT YOU'LL DO:

1. Preheat the oven to 325°.

2. Cut the livers into approximately one-inch squares or mash and shape them into one-inch diameter balls and place on an ungreased cookie sheet.

3. Bake for 45 minutes.

3. Let dry, uncovered, for at least 24 hours.

Makes approximately 24 liver treats.

Dinners

McRice 'N' Grub

Who doesn't like fast food every once in a while? Did somebody say Mc-Dog-alds?

Note: When preparing the vegetables, throw a slice of carrot your dog's way. If you're lucky, he will love it! You can use carrots to add variety to your dog's treat regimen. They're a good source of vitamin A, and some studies suggest they help dogs' sense of smell.

WHAT YOU'LL NEED:

- 2 cups uncooked brown rice
- ¹/₂ pound raw ground turkey or ground beef
- 1 teaspoon olive oil
- 1 clove garlic, chopped (trust us: it's better than garbage breath)
- ¹/₂ cup carrots, broccoli, or spinach, chopped into half-inch pieces
- 4 cups water

Prep. time: 15 minutes
Cooking time: approximately 1 hour

WHAT YOU'LL DO:

1. Combine all ingredients in a large pot and boil, covered, until all the water has been absorbed (approximately one hour).

2. Let cool. Serve in bowls along with a bowl of fresh cold water.

Makes 2 medium-sized dinners.

Thanksgiving Dinner

Most dog owners have at one time or another made an attempt to treat their beloved pets to something special during the holidays. We want them to celebrate with us, to know that it is a special time. Once, we gave our dog a piece of matzo ball so he could celebrate Passover with us, and although he enjoyed grandma's recipe, I don't think he grasped the holiday's full meaning.

Try this recipe. Our dogs may not know what Thanksgiving means to us, but they will certainly know it means good eats for them!

Note: This recipe can be used on any major holiday, but the less frequently it is served, the greater the dog's memory of the occasion. At least, we like to think so.

WHAT YOU'LL NEED:

- 2 pounds ground turkey
- 2 eggs
- 2 cups cooked brown rice
- 3 carrots, diced
- 1 apple, diced

Prep. time: 15 minutes
Cooking time: 45 minutes

WHAT YOU'LL DO:

1. Preheat the oven to 375°.

2. Combine all of the ingredients in a mixing bowl.

3. Divide mixture in half. On a cookie sheet, mold it into shapes (we like to make a Turkey, but our dogs seem to prefer the Pilgrims)

4. Bake for 45 minutes.

5. Let cool.

Makes 2 Turkey (or one Pilgrim and one Indian) dinners.

Desserts and Special Snacks

Desserts and snacks for dogs, as for people, should be eaten in moderation. For large dogs especially, weight problems can equal health problems. We recommend saving rich desserts and fattening snacks for very special occasions, such as birthdays, holidays, or after teeth cleanings.

Liver Birthday Cake

WHAT YOU'LL NEED:

- 1/2 pound chicken livers
- 2 tablespoons olive oil
- 1/2 cup of water
- 1/2 pound ground beef or turkey
- 2 cups of flour

Prep. time: 15 minutes
Cooking time: 90 minutes,
plus time to cool
Decorating time: 20 minutes

WHAT YOU'LL DO:

Cake

1. Preheat the oven to 350°.

2. Puree the liver, oil, and water in a blender. Set aside 1/2 cup of the mixture.

3. Combine the remaining mixture with the ground beef or turkey. Add the flour and mix into a batter.

4. Pour or spoon the mixture into an ungreased cake pan and bake for 1 and 1/2 hours (or until well-done).

5. Let cool completely before decorating.

Frosting

Add a touch of food coloring (color determined by the holiday) to the 1/2 cup of reserved mixture and place it in a plastic baggie. Cut off a corner of the baggie and squeeze the mixture onto the cake, spelling out a celebratory message.

Peanut Butter Balls

Finally, a treat we can share with our dogs.

Note: Pills can be easily hidden in peanut butter balls. Serve on a spoon or on bread and have lots of water on hand afterward.

WHAT YOU'LL NEED:

- 1 cup smooth peanut butter
- $1/4$ cup honey

Prep time: 25 minutes
Cooking time: none

WHAT YOU'LL DO:

1. Mix the peanut butter and honey in a large mixing bowl.

2. Shape mixture into $1/2$-inch balls.

3. Let sit for 15 minutes and serve. Peanut butter balls can be served when they're still warm.

Any extra peanut butter balls should be refrigerated.

Doggy Cheese Bites

Yum. Doggies don't have to wait for a piece of cheese to drop off the counter with these delectable desserts.

WHAT YOU'LL NEED:

- 4 cups all-purpose flour
- 2 ¹/₂ cups cheddar cheese, shredded
- ¹/₂ teaspoon garlic powder
- 1 cup olive oil
- ¹/₂ cup water

Prep. time: 20 minutes
Cooking time: 15 minutes

WHAT YOU'LL DO:

1. Combine the flour, cheese, garlic, and olive oil in a large bowl.

2. Mix together thoroughly, then add the water.

3. Shape contents into a log and cut slices about ³/₄ of an inch thick. Place on ungreased cookie sheets and bake at 350° for 15 minutes.

4. Let cool completely before serving.

Lynyrd's Inyrds

Use this recipe after making a Sunday roaster chicken.

Note: Do not feed neckbone to your dog or anyone else. Pull all the meat from the bone before serving.

WHAT YOU'LL NEED:

- Chicken innards (you know, the stuff in the middle of the bird)

WHAT YOU'LL DO:

1. Place the innards in a heavy skillet. Fill with water until the innards are just covered.

2. Simmer the innards for 20 minutes.

3. Let cool. Slice and serve as a Sunday treat.

Doggy First Aid

Few things make us feel more helpless than being unable to take care of our sick or injured dog. When it comes to Doggy First Aid, the Boy Scout motto "be prepared" just might save a dog's life.

Of course, the best course of action for a sick or injured pet is always to take him to a vet, but sometimes this may not be immediately possible. Doggy First Aid is for emergency, in-the-field care and should always be followed by a vet visit.

Assessment

The first step you should take at the scene of an accident or injury is to secure yourself and the dog. If he is lying in the road, be sure that you will be safe from oncoming traffic when you go to treat him.

▶ Quickly examine his condition to see if he is conscious or unconscious.

▶ Check to see if he is bleeding or having seizures.

▶ Check your dog's breathing. If he is unconscious, watch his chest to see if it rises and falls.

▸ Check your dog's pulse by placing a few fingers on the inside of his hind leg, at the joint with his body.

▸ Check your dog's gums. Healthy gums will be pinkish. If your dog is in shock or has poor circulation, his gums may be grayish.

Response

If he is not breathing, but has a pulse, perform mouth-to-mouth.

1. **Check for apparent neck or back injuries before you begin. If none are visibly apparent, tilt your dog's neck back slightly to open his air passage.**

2. **Hold his mouth firmly closed. Try to make an airtight seal.**

3. **Put your mouth over his nose—over his nose and mouth if he is a smaller dog—and gently blow air into his lungs for a few seconds. DO NOT force air into his lungs, especially with smaller dogs.**

4. **Take a breath and repeat at three- to five-second intervals.**

5. **Check your dog's chest between breaths. Continue mouth-to-mouth until you see him breathing.**

If he is not breathing and does not have a pulse, perform CPR:

1. **Check for apparent neck or back injuries. If none are apparent, gently roll your dog onto his right side.**

2. **Kneel so that his back is to you.**

3. **For large dogs:** Put your hands together and lock your fingers. Place your hands to the left of the widest part of his chest just below the elbow. Compress (about one to three inches) and release. If you are alone, alternate compressions with a mouth-to-mouth breath. If you have a helper, you should compress while he or she performs mouth-to-mouth. Perform five compressions to every mouth-to-mouth breath if your dog weighs 30 to 90 pounds. Perform ten compressions for every breath for dogs weighing over 90 pounds.

   For small dogs: Place your hand around the dog's chest. Place one hand on the widest part of his chest just below the elbow, and the other hand under the right side of his chest. Compress (about 1 inch) and release the left side of his chest. Perform five compressions to every mouth-to-mouth breath.

4. **After a couple of minutes, check your dog's pulse. Continue CPR until you feel his pulse.**

   Once you have restored your dog's breathing and pulse, get to a vet immediately. Use common sense when it comes to treating your dog for other injuries on the way to the vet.

   ▶ If you move a dog with a neck or back injury, you could paralyze him for life. Carefully slide a board under the dog before you move him.

   ▶ If your dog is bleeding, use a clean cloth to apply direct pressure on the wound to help slow or stop the bleeding.

   ▶ Dogs can go into shock just as humans do. Try to keep your pooch warm and calm.

Holi-days

Whether you live with Rufus Claus or Hanukkah Bella, what holiday isn't—or can't be made—dog friendly? (Okay, maybe Yom Kippur isn't all that much doggy fun. But it's not supposed to be fun.)

Holidays with your dog don't have to be a battle. You don't have to lock your dog outside when the family is tearing into Christmas presents. You don't have to close your dog in the basement when trick-or-treaters come to the door. All you have to do to enjoy the holidays with your doggy is include him!

In this chapter you'll find all kinds of activities that revolve around making good doggy fun for the big holidays. After all, your dog is part of the family, and being with family is the best part of celebrating holidays. These activities are sure to bring a smile to your doggy's lips.

New Year's Eve

With seven dog years to every human year, Rufus should celebrate New Year's Eve much more often, but on December 31 you can celebrate with him. Beyond the typical New Year's stroll, you and Rufus can make up an evening of New Year's fun (but please, no champagne).

Resolutions

It's a good idea for you and Rufus to write out his New Year's resolutions before the clock strikes twelve. Unless he's grown an opposable thumb, he'll need your help to think them up and write them down. Here are a few ideas to get you started.

I, Rufus, will try to do whatever my owner says—as long as he speaks Dog.

I, Rufus, will stop jumping on people when they come to the door.

I, Rufus, will cut down to two cats a day—any more than that may be hazardous to my health.

I, Rufus, will refuse to beg for table scraps—they don't help my figure anyway.

You get the picture.

Don't be too disappointed if Rufus doesn't stick to his resolutions during the year. Who does?

Easter/Passover

The joyous spring holidays means time again to run in the open fields, sniff every newly marked tree, roll in dewy grass, and, of course, celebrate Easter or Passover.

Our dogs experience a "rebirth," a new start when spring comes. They get to show off their spring haircuts, chase the returning birds, and hunt for the bones they buried last fall, which got covered by all that cold, wet, white stuff.

WHAT YOU'LL NEED:

- Bones, liver treats, or chopped liver on matzo
- New chew toys, new tennis balls, or old socks
- Some hiding places

WHAT YOU'LL DO:

The equivalent of an Easter egg hunt or Passover "find the Afikomen" game.

Warning: If you have children and are running a chocolate Easter egg hunt, be sure that all of the chocolate has been picked up before your dog gets to look for his treats. Chocolate can be fatal for canines!

1. Prepare your treats. Liver treats are generally the most delectable and easiest to find. If you're running an Easter Bone hunt, hide each bone with a liver treat (see p. 99). If you're running a Find the Doggy-komen game, spread a little chopped liver on a few pieces of matzo and keep that near the bones. (Usually, there's only one Afikomen, but it's more fun for your doggy if you distribute the Doggy-komen around the house.)

2. The night before, while your dog is sleeping, hide his bones around the house.

3. The next morning take your doggy on his hunt. Feel free to help him out a little bit: first let him smell the kind of bone he's looking for.

If that's not enough:

Easter: Prepare a basket of treats for your doggy. Be sure to keep him from eating the plastic Easter grass, though. Try replacing it with some real crab grass!

Passover: At the Seder, when you open the door for Elijah, give a quiet whistle. When your four-legged friend trots through the door, he's sure to be a hit!

Fourth of July

Okay, for some dogs the Fourth is not such a dog-friendly holiday. Many dogs hate a night filled with loud explosions. But there are some alternatives.

▶ Stay home and comfort your dog.

▶ Take your dog to the barbeque with you and comfort her there.

▶ If you have to leave her alone, turn on Animal Planet or a like-minded station and turn the volume way up.

For those of you with braver pooches:

▶ Take Bella to the barbeque and show off some of her tricks.

▶ Train her to drop and play dead every time a firecracker goes off.

▶ Gather some of your friends and their doggy compadres and play some games (see Games, p. 36).

▶ Line up a row of sparklers to make a doggy raceway.

Halloween

Warning! Chocolate consumption can kill your dog. Be very careful and aware of what your dog picks up on Halloween night.

Halloween is a good time not only to walk the dog, but also to coordinate her outfit—with you or your child! Many dogs don't take so well to masks, but fun headbands and sunglasses sometimes work.

Try these person-dog costume pairings. Whenever possible, add sunglasses.

Charlie Brown and Snoopy. Blockhead will be a hit as he and his white-and-black painted canine (with special floppy-eared headband) knock on the door for treats. (Although, with Charlie's luck, no one will have any bones for Snoopy.)

The Grinch and his dog Max. We recommend saving this costume for Christmas. But if you can't wait, all you need is a Grinch costume for you and a horn headband for Rufus. (If only the good doctor had written *The Grinch Who Stole All-Hallows Eve*.)

Han Solo or Princess Leia with Chewbacca. It is harder to make the Han Solo or Princess Leia costume than it is make your dog look like Chewbacca, especially if he's already brown and hairy. If you want, you can strap a black belt around your dog's chest and let him carry the "laser ammo."

Little Bo Peep and her sheep. Your child can herd a sheep from house to house. If you don't have a border collie or a sheepdog, try tying a loose-stranded mop top around her head. A matching cotton coat covered in pieces of shag carpet completes the outfit.

Little Miss Muffet and the spider. Some extra legs made out of foam pipe insulation taped to your dog's cotton coat will scare more than just Miss Muffet away.

Native American with a buffalo. The warrior Native American missed his mark—or so it seems, when you put a Steve Martin-esque "arrow through the head" headband over Rufus's rump.

Winnie the Pooh and Tigger, too. A tiger-striped coat (see Doggy Clothing, p. 8) and socks may not automatically give your dog the bounce of Tigger, but your pup will help Winnie get his hand out of the honey jar!

Thanksgiving

When celebrating the fall harvest with your doggy, it's tempting to slide scraps of turkey and gravy off the table. This is fine when done in moderation, but Thanksgiving table scraps can make Bella very ill. We have some alternate suggestions that will help her enjoy Thanksgiving in a more healthy way.

Warning: Do not feed your dogs turkey bones. Poultry bones are very soft and may splinter, lodging in your dog's throat or colon. For the most part, dogs have been domesticated so much that their systems can no longer support the consumption of such bones. So please, BE CAREFUL!

Cook up a fine "Doggy Thanksgiving Dinner" or "Lynyrd's Inyrds" (see Cooking for Your Dog, p. 98). When it comes to feeding time, let her sit under the table.

If you really like to feed her table scraps and you have a large family, take turns. Mom gets to feed Bella turkey. Dad gets to feed her stuffing. The kids get to feed her a very small taste of pie. This way, everyone gets to share in her Thanksgiving and she doesn't get overfed or sick.

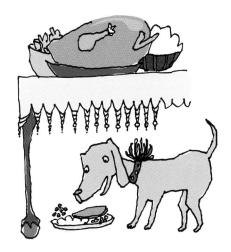

Let your dog play in the family football/soccer game. You may have to change the rules a little bit for the times when Bella picks up the ball and makes you chase her for ten minutes, but that's all part of the fun!

Christmas/Hanukkah/Kwanzaa

The winter holidays are by far the most doggy enjoyable. For starters, if your dog is Jewish, he has eight nights of presents and latke table scraps to enjoy. For Christmas, it's one big day of ham or turkey, stockings, and ribbon. Kwanzaa provides seven days of carrot salad and succotash.

But the food is just the beginning. Santa hats tied around your dog's head or playing dreidl for dog biscuits always helps to enhance the holiday spirit (of course you'll have to spin for your dog).

And then there are the presents. Here is a list of some suggestions for celebrating the winter holidays with your doggy.

▶ Leave a bone and small bowl of water out for Doggy Claus. (Someone will eat it . . .)

▶ Prepare stockings for your dog. Dinosaur-sized bones, new rubber candy canes, or a pair of your old socks make great stocking stuffers.

▶ Wrap a new shirt for Rufus for the third night of Hanukkah.

▶ Take a long walk spent reflecting on the meaning of your own and your dog's life while you celebrate Kwanzaa.

When the food comes out . . . well, to each his own. We like to share the turkey and latkes on the holidays in moderation. They only come once every seven dog years.

Further holiday celebrations:

▶ Dress yourself up as the Grinch and your dog as his pet Max (see Halloween, p. 113).

▶ Make cards for your dogs to send to their friends (see Holiday Cards, p. 19).

▹ Make ornaments, menorahs, or kinari with pictures of your dog or his paw print (see Dog Prints, p. 18).

▹ Send your dog's park pals a homemade bone wrapped in a ribbon (see Cooking for Your Dog, p. 98).

Holiday Gifts:

▹ A huge dinosaur-sized bone

▹ Booties for hiking

▹ Trekking jackets

▹ A new collar

▹ Old socks

▹ New tennis balls

▹ Slippers (that he can chew without being yelled at!)

Birthdays

What better annual celebration to share with your doggy every year than a birthday party—or seven! For those of you who know when your dog's birthday is, skip ahead to the "What You'll Need" section; for those of you who have no idea when your dog was born, follow these easy steps to selecting a Doggy Birthday:

- ▶ Have your vet do a dental check to estimate your dog's age
- ▶ Pick a month or an astrological sign that you think fits your dog's personality
- ▶ Pick a day within that month or sign and make it your dog's birthday!

Alternatively, you can make your dog's birthday the day you found her or picked her up from the pound.

WHAT YOU'LL NEED:

- Invitations (see Holiday Cards, p. 19)
- Tennis balls
- Party favors
- Liver Birthday Cake (see p. 103)
- A large, shallow bucket or kiddie pool (optional)

WHAT YOU'LL DO:

1. First you need to decide whether you are having an indoor or an outdoor party. In some cases, of course, the weather will be a determining factor. The dog park, your own backyard, or a friend's house with a pool (with lowered chlorine levels for doggy swimming) are all great locations!

2. Find out how many of your doggy's friends are coming. Make a list of the dogs your pooch likes to play, wrestle, or sniff with.

3. Make invitations and send them out.

4. Run events at the party:

   ▹ Bob for tennis balls in a bucket or kiddie pool filled with water.

   ▹ If you have access to a pool, lower the chlorine levels and let the dogs swim the day away. This might also be a good time for the other dog owners to give their pooches baths, so be sure to provide shampoo and towels!

   ▹ Play games, including To the Tree and Back (see p. 36) and The Fastest Fetcher in the West (see p. 38).

   ▹ Give prizes for your events: pet store gift certificates, rubber chew toys, and bones all work wonders at a doggy party.

   ▹ Let them eat cake. The Liver Birthday Cake is the perfect capper to a doggy birthday. Just be sure that your dog shares with the other dogs.

Chances are, after the party both you and your pooch will be sleeping the day away. And if you're not too tired, you can throw another party again in a few months.

Birthday Gift Ideas

Many of us have received a Father's Day, birthday, or Christmas gift from our pooch. And who hasn't shed some love on her doggy with a new chew toy, rubber bone, or new dog bed? There is one group, however, that is often left out of the doggy gift loop: your dog's friends!

With a little time, love, and help from you, your dog can give the gift of love to any dog she wants. She'll be the most loved dog on the block.

WHAT YOU'LL NEED:

- Access to a "paint-it-yourself" ceramic store
- Homemade dog bones (see p. 98)
- Maps of your favorite hikes or walks (highlight fire hydrants, cat houses, and extra-large trees)
- Dog-treat recipes printed on index cards
- Doggy toys
- Pet store gift certificates

WHAT YOU'LL DO:

Most cities have a "paint-it-yourself" ceramic store where you can design personalized pottery. The idea, once you get there, is to create a gift bowl for your dog's friends.

▸ Hand-paint ornaments with your doggy's friends' names on them.

▸ Personalize food and water bowls (you'll fill these with all the other goodies).

▸ Paint a treats jar with the dog's favorite treats. Write "Good Girl Treats" on a sticker to label the special jar!

Once you have your personalized ceramics, it's time to fill them up! Fill the treat jar with homemade dog bones and your favorite dog treat recipe. Arrange the treat jar, ornaments, hiking maps, and other favors in the dog bowl. Cover it tightly in plastic wrap to ensure that the dog doesn't get to the treats before it's time.

Mix up the combinations of these gifts to give to your own pooch, or for your pooch to give to you. And remember, it's not the gift, it's the sniff that counts!

Resources

For general doggy information:

animalnetwork.com

dogomania.com

thepoop.com

Artsy Days

For your doggy building needs:

wood-worker.com/plans/doghouse

For your doggy reading needs:

dogbooks.com

For your doggy clothing needs:

kaynyne.com

For your doggy poetry and quotable needs:

kerryblues.org

Indoors-y and Outdoors-y Days

For a serious doggy aptitude test:

golden-retriever.com

For your doggy fun needs:

caninegames.com

dog-play.com

For your doggy massage, first aid, and other needs:

learnfree-pets.com

For your doggy training needs:

doglogic.com

Travel, Healthy, and Holi-days

For lists of national dog-welcoming restaurants, hotels, and parks:

dogfriendly.com

For information about the Texas Fire Museum (site of the largest fire hydrant in America):

texasfiremuseum.com

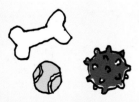